# Reflections

## Biblical And Otherwise, On Sexuality

Edited by

Catherine Clark Kroeger

and

Tina J. Ostrander

Reformation Press

Reformation Press
P.O. Box 2210
136 Tremont Park Drive
Lenoir, North Carolina 28645


Reformation Press books, monographs and other resources are available at special discounts in bulk purchases for educational and ministry use. For more details, contact:


Director of Publications
Reformation Press
P.O. Box 2210
136 Tremont Park Drive
Lenoir, North Carolina 28645


Printed in the United States of America

# Contents

# Preface

On the streets, there were few people from whom I could ask directions that early Saturday morning. Somehow, I found the church tucked away on a back street in the middle of the block.

I crawled wearily out of the car after a drive of more than 200 miles. I had left home at four o'clock in the morning and now, as I approached the church, I wondered why I had bothered to come at all. I was becoming something of a fixture at area meetings of various mainline religious denominations that were studying sexual issues. Why, I fumed to myself, was it worth the effort to present a viewpoint that few seemed anxious to accept?

Inside the warm church basement, I received a gracious welcome from the denominational representative who had invited me. I had been surprised, when he first called me with the invitation, at the relief which he expressed when I agreed to come.

I now posed to him the same question that I had asked myself earlier: Why in the world did he want a person from another denomination to speak on sexual issues from a conservative perspective?

He answered as he had before: that, while many were eager to address the topic from a more liberal stance, few people were willing to make a presentation that would deal with the biblical material in an academic manner.

I protested that I knew of a local church that would gladly have supplied speakers with a "before and after" testimony

"Our people want to deal with what's in the Bible," he replied. "Fifteen percent have taken one side of the argument, and they are very militant in expressing it. Another 15 percent are firmly on the other side and just as aggressive in their approach. In the middle are 70 percent who are really looking for guidance on the subject."

Suddenly, I understood his position. The people of God earnestly were seeking guidance on their path through a murky issue; and they were beset by passion and politics on both sides.

What was needed was a dispassionate exposition of relevant material, without mudslinging, name calling or outbursts of emotion. Those who came with open hearts and minds frequently were deflected by attitudes, expressions and actions that were unbecoming of those who belong to Jesus Christ.

Was it possible to present an understanding of the Bible's precepts in a way that was respectful of all people as well as faithful to Scripture?

Was it possible to sense the deep pain that some brought with them and the longing for healing of the wounds?

Could one address the militants of both parties with a moderate and rational voice?

Could we center on the will of God rather than the animosities of human beings?

How could the Bible be employed, not as a weapon of war, but as a light to our way and a lamp to our feet?

In answer to those questions, this endeavor was born.This book was intended to widely make available material that might help to inform each of us in the decisions that must be made in our own lives and conduct, in our homes and in our churches. At the heart of our reflections is our understanding of the nature and appropriate use of Scripture.

In a public debate with me, Victor Paul Furnish once announced that "the fundamental difference between me and Dr. Kroeger is our position on the interpretation of the Bible."

Of course, he was right. This book is an effort to speak in irenic tones to those seeking to understand the thinking of people committed to the authority and inspiration of Scripture. Our purpose was to prepare materials that might open up honest discussions that would be characterized by dignity and decency.

Catherine Clark Kroeger
Cape Cod Institute for Christian Studies
Brewster, Massachusetts
May 2001

# CHAPTER 1

# To Ask a Better Question

## *The Heterosexuality-Homosexuality Debate Revisited*

### Mary Stewart Van Leeuwen

*W*hat might a centrist analysis of sexuality look
like at a time when churches are awash in
disputes over the meaning and implications
*of sexual orientation? Reclaiming the center of faith
involves taking a critical look at both sides of the
debate over same-sex unions and the ordination of
homosexuals. The time has come to move beyond the
nature-nurture debate and address the larger question
of how Christians can rise above the sexual chaos of
our age through sexual discipline and protection of the
vulnerable.*

Various mainline and evangelical movements now are
working to reclaim the center of Christian faith after many
decades of living with an oversimplified "right versus left"
portrait of church life.

Other authors in this issue (*Interpretation* April 1997)
have examined theological, ecclesiological and philosophical
implications of these movements, but surely all would agree
that practical theological concerns also should be addressed.

What might a centrist analysis of sexuality look like at a time when churches are awash in disputes over the meaning and implications of sexual orientation? The following is one Calvinist centrist's attempt to answer this question.

Let me begin with some clarifying remarks about my background and approach to this topic. My professional expertise is in psychology and philosophy, making me at best a self-trained theologian and Biblical scholar. I think it will be most useful if I first use my professional resources to make several points about the definition of sexual orientation and the controversy surrounding its origins. Quite simply, it is inadvisable to change policy regarding gays and lesbians in the church – including their ordination and the blessing of their unions – until such issues are clarified.

Second, I come to this task as a recent participant in two ecumenical and interdisciplinary projects: the Religion, Culture, and Family Project (based at the University of Chicago Divinity School and sponsored by the Lilly Foundation), and the Welfare Responsibility Project (based at the Center for Public Justice in Washington and sponsored by the Pew Charitable Trusts).

Both these efforts have convinced me that two deeper and more serious issues underlie the heterosexuality-homosexuality debate: our culture's romanticization of sexual libertarianism, which in turn is symptomatic of a second and more foundational problem, which I call "Enlightenment individualism run wild."

My conviction is that, until both these revolutions (sexuality and individualism) have bottomed out and the church has repented of its complicity in both kinds of idolatry, it is in no position to be throwing stones at gays, but also in no position to make hasty decisions about their future in the church.

Thus, instead of dwelling on questions about the permissibility of ordaining or blessing the unions of self-identified gays, the "better question" I want to pose is this:

*"What must all who follow Christ be prepared to do in*

*order to move beyond the sexual chaos of our culture and build churches and communities that truly are humane?"*

## Clarifying Some Terms

For convenience, I already have used the dichotomous terms homosexuality-heterosexuality and gay-straight. And yet, as C.P. Snow observed more than three decades ago in a different context, "The number two is a very dangerous number. Attempts to divide anything into two ought to be regarded with much suspicion."[1]

Most people now know that the term "homosexuality" – and the related notion of a fixed sexual orientation – emerged only in the context of 19th century Western intellectual discourse. Some advocates for the empowerment of gays in the church have made much of this fact, stating, for example, that the Apostle Paul's strictures against same-sex relationships were made in ignorance of the biological determinants of sexual orientation and, therefore, should be applied only to heterosexuals who perversely act against their own natural inclinations.

> If defining homosexuality is controversial, settling the question as to its causality is doubly so.
>
> Most mainline church study documents on the issue simply assume that its biological origins are scientifically established, but this is far from the case.

But my own position is almost the reverse. I think our Old Testament and New Testament ancestors were correct in treating homosexual acts (along with fornication, adultery, incest and even bestiality) as behaviors to which *any* person potentially could be tempted, and that is why they remind their readers to be on guard against all of them.

It may seem that I view sexuality as having the same origin and degree of plasticity as our language capacity. Some psycholinguists have theorized that infants are biologically "pre-wired" to learn the deep grammar that underlies all human languages – pre-wired to develop an understanding of syntax that includes nouns and adjectives, subject-predicate agreements, verb tenses and so on – simply by virtue of having enough exposure to a given language community early in life.

What *particular* household tongue a child learns depends on the language community to which she or he is exposed. But all biologically normal infants have this brain-based language-processing mechanism waiting to be "committed" to a particular household tongue and, after such neurological commitment, there progressively is less likelihood that fluency can be developed in other languages.

Is the development of sexual orientation similar? Do we all come "pre-wired" for sensual and, eventually, orgasmic response to a potentially wide range of triggering objects, which then are narrowed down by our critical-period experiences so that we end up "committed" to hetero-, homo- or bisexuality?

This is more or less what Freud meant when he theorized that infants were "polymorphously perverse." In Freud's view, the sexuality of infants is totally undifferentiated and directed toward a wide range of targets until it gradually is channeled in socially appropriate directions. Thus, he concluded, all human beings inherently are bisexual; that is, potentially capable both of homosexual and heterosexual behavior.

We can see why Freud's theory might seem at least partially plausible when we stop to ask the question, "Just how prevalent is homosexuality in the population?" The answer, it turns out, depends on how the term is defined.

In random-sample surveys, such as the landmark *Sex in America* study,[2] when homosexuality narrowly is defined – either by self-identity or by sexual contact exclusively with same-sex partners in the past year – then less than 3 percent of adult men and 2 percent of women are homosexual. When it is defined in terms of ever having had a same-sex contact, the percentages go up to about 9 percent and 4 percent, respectively.

These figures are complicated, however, by the fact that for upwards of half the *men* who report having had any same-sex contact, it occurred before age 18 and never again thereafter, whereas *women* who report same-sex contact usually had it after age 18.

If homosexuality is defined, even more widely, as ongoing attraction to same-sex persons or to same-sex erotic activities (regardless of one's feelings or behavior with the other sex), then the figures in America are close to 5 percent for men and women alike.

Finally, if it is defined as ever having had a same-sex erotic fantasy in one's lifetime (whether acted upon or not), then the figures for both men and women are in the 10 percent range.

These figures certainly play havoc with any theory that sees sexual orientation as a clear-cut biological dichotomy. And, yet, it is precisely to such an implicit theory (often assumed to be empirically corroborated and scientifically uncontroversial) that many biblical scholars, theologians and writers of denominational study reports appeal when they claim that the biblical writers knew nothing about the "biological origins" of homosexuality.

Because the *Sex in America* survey yields only correlational data, its authors caution that their work cannot directly address the nature-nurture question regarding the origins of homosexuality. They go on, however, to say that:

> Our findings are relevant to how that debate might proceed. If any nature theory is based on a constant proportion of the population being "homosexual," our findings suggest that proportion is very small, and that the status may change for individuals from one age to

another.

More important, both those who have a nature as well as a nurture point of view will be required to identify more precisely what homosexuality is. Is it attraction, behavior or identity that these theorists predict, or is it some combination of the three? And is the combination the same in women and men? These debates have enough politics in them to assure that no single study will settle the matter.[3]

These authors are right in saying that this is more than just an esoteric scientific debate. With more and more pressure for the recognition of same-sex domestic partnerships or marriages, the issue has wide-ranging legal, economic and childrearing ramifications.

> The human biological program is biased toward heterosexuality and, as a species, we are not infinitely malleable in terms of our potential sexual orientation.
> One can explain this in terms of sociobiology, or natural theology, or both. But we cannot ignore the evidence for the normative pattern.

And yet, our society continues to yield to such pressure (and groups within the church continue to lobby for the ordination of homosexuals and the blessing of their unions) in the midst of a definitional confusion that benefits no one. When so much is at stake regarding the future shape of church and society, this is a questionable way to proceed.

## The Nature-Nurture Debate Revisited

If defining homosexuality is controversial, settling the question as to its causality is doubly so. Most mainline church study documents on the issue simply assume that its biological origins are scientifically established, but this is far from the case.

To begin with, establishing causality requires a broadly accepted definition of just what it is we are observing and, as we already have seen, such consensus is lacking. Is sexual orientation dichotomous or a continuum between gay and straight? If the latter, what constitutes "threshold" homosexuality? Do we determine this according to behavior, self-professed identity, fantasy life, degree of attraction to others, or some combination of the above? By which criteria do we decide, for purposes of scientific investigation (not to mention social policy decisions), how to operationalize our definitions of "gay" and "straight?"

The blunt truth, in the words of one reviewer of the literature, is that "a clear and unambiguous method of classifying people as homosexual or heterosexual does not exist."[4]

The result of such definitional confusion often is careless science compounded by bad science journalism. The much-quoted finding of Simon LeVay on the smaller size of a certain hypothalamic nucleus in gay as opposed to straight men, for example, was based on a comparison of the post-mortem brains of men who had or had not died of AIDS.[5] It simply was assumed that this was sufficient to distinguish the two samples as gay or straight – a dubious assumption, since some actively gay men do not get AIDS and some actively straight men do.

Moreover, the differences in hypothalamic size between the two groups only was an average difference, which means that some of the so-called gay men had normal-sized nuclei and some of the so-called straight men had smaller nuclei.

Finally, LeVay's research is only correlational, not experimental; thus, we do not know (even had the differences been more clear-cut) whether it is differing brains that cause differing sexual orientations or vice versa since experience does change the brain throughout life. By the time the study reached many newspapers, however, it had been translated into a clear-cut, biologically caused difference between two clearly defined samples of people.

Similar problems of interpretation plague attempts to establish hormonal and genetic differences between so-called gay and straight samples. In a 1991 report, for example, Bailey and Pillard sought out self-identified gay men (most of them from twin pairs) and then counted the number of their male siblings who also were gay. They found that more than 50 percent of the sample's identical co-twins, but only 22 percent of fraternal co-twins and 11 percent of adoptive brothers, were self-identified gays.[6]

Since identical twins share all of their genes, whereas fraternal twins share only about 50 percent and adoptive twins even fewer, these differing rates of concordance for homosexuality were seen as indirect evidence for the existence of a "gay gene."

But this conclusion ignores the fact that identical twins share more similar environments throughout childhood than other sibling pairs. Unlike most fraternal twin pairs (let alone ordinary siblings), identical twins look alike, and often are dressed alike and treated alike by parents, teachers and other adults.

To disentangle the effects of nature and nurture, one must look at identical twins who have been *raised separately,* then see how similar they remain on a given behavioral trait despite their different environments.

It is difficult to find separated pairs of identical twins of any sort, let alone pairs that include at least one self-identified homosexual, but the one study of six such pairs found *only one* of the pairs was concordant for homosexual identity. This is a percentage not much higher than that of the adoptive brother pairs in the Bailey and Pillard study and, thus, calls into question their earlier conclusion about a genetic basis for homosexuality.

Even when chromosomes are directly examined, the evidence for a "gay gene" is equivocal. A 1993 study that looked at 40 homosexual brother pairs found 64 percent of the pairs shared an identical section of DNA on the X chromosome –

higher than the statistical likelihood of 50 percent for siblings in general.

This, again, was taken as possible evidence for the existence of a "gay gene." The researchers, however, did not bother to look at the genes of any heterosexual brothers of the homosexual pairs to see if they shared the same genetic marker. Without such a control, the study's findings remain inconclusive.[7]

These studies represent only a few of the many that have been done on the relationship of brain structure, hormones and genes to homosexuality,[8] but they exemplify the methodological problems in determining the biological bases of sexual orientation. These problems, when added to the confusion on definitions, make it doubly advisable for churches to proceed slowly and cautiously with any changes in doctrine and ecclesiology relating to homosexuals.

## Between Dualism and Biological Reductionism

How, then, should we proceed to understand sexual orientation and its ethical implications?

Let me suggest that the Freudian theory of sexual-orientation plasticity *and* its opposite (the view that sexual orientation is biologically and immutably fixed in the same manner as eye color or handedness) are both too simple: the first because it does not take biology seriously enough, and the second because it takes biology *too* seriously – or, more accurately, because it appeals to biology in too reductionist a manner. Let me briefly criticize each of these approaches before laying out an alternative.

Regarding the first, or "under-biologizing," error, recall my earlier analogy between Freud's theory about plasticity of potential sexual orientation and Chomsky's theory of language acquisition. The limits of that analogy become apparent when we remember that our complex language capacity represents a great *difference* between us and other mammals, whereas our reproductive anatomy and physiology develop in a more *similar* fashion. This is one reason why attempts to understand the biology of both male/femaleness and hetero/homosexuality can include studies using rats, sheep, monkeys and other animals. Another reason is that experimental manipulations can be done on animals that would be unethical if performed on humans.

Along with clinical observations of human beings whose bio-sexual development departs from the norm, such studies have shown what a complex process underlies the mere development of male and female sexual anatomy and physiology, let alone sexual orientation.

There is a feminist slogan to the effect that "Adam was God's rough draft." Viewed from one angle, this turns out to be truer than the slogan's originators probably knew because standard male bio-sexual development *in utero* proceeds rather like the building of a Rube Goldberg machine. Various things get added for which there are no analogs in the more efficient female model – and this, incidentally, means that more can go wrong in the male developmental process.

To borrow a metaphor from a computer manual, it appears that God's original "default option" was to produce a female. That is, from undifferentiated embryonic structures – regardless of chromosomal maleness or femaleness – an anatomically female body will emerge *unless* these successive male "add-ons" arrive during critical periods of fetal development. In a playful warning against overly literalist readings of Genesis 2, these "add-ons" have been collectively referred to as the "Adam principle."

We now know that a major factor in all of this is testosterone, a hormone produced by both sexes but in ratios that differ, on average, at different times in pre- and postnatal development. Critical levels of testosterone are implicated in prenatal male anatomical development, including not just sexual structures in the pelvic region, but sexual differentiation of the hypothalamus in the brain. At puberty, another critical rise in testosterone levels leads to the emergence of male second-ary sex characteristics. From puberty on, testosterone levels influence sexual arousability in both men and women.

And in animals, postnatal testosterone levels strongly are connected to levels of aggression in male and female alike. More intriguingly, if one artificially interferes with testos-terone levels in various animals in their mid-prenatal devel-opment (eliminating it in males or increasing it above a cer-tain level in females), the result often will be cross-sex play behavior after they are born and cross-sex mating behavior when they become adults.

Clearly, biology does matter, and it follows a predictable if complicated course. The biological aspects of sex-uality (e.g., chromoso-mal, gonadal, hormonal, anatomical) usually cor-respond with each other and with psychological aspects (e.g., gender identity, erotic orienta-tion) to lead to male-female sexual bonding and subsequent repro-ductive activity.

> Today's church needs to recover a high view of sexual discipline – not primarily to pander to ancient purity codes, but to embody the enduring biblical norm of protecting the vulnerable and integrating them into the community.

The concordance of these multiple aspects *can* break down on rare occasions; indeed, although still a matter of debate, the fact that men's bio-sexual development prenatally is more complex (and, hence, more vulnerable to error) than women's *may* help to explain why self-identified gays not only out-number lesbians but also are more likely to report having felt that they were "different" from a very early age.

But the norm is clear: The human biological program is biased toward heterosexuality and, as a species, we are not infinitely malleable in terms of our potential sexual orienta-tion. One can explain this in terms of sociobiology, or natural theology, or both. But we cannot ignore the evidence for the normative pattern.

What about the second, or "biological reductionist," error?

If, as I have just argued, the biological norm for our species is so stable and even if departures from it are becoming understandable as biological processes gone wrong, does this not make biology destiny?

The best answer to this question is "yes" and "no." Crude sociobiology to the contrary, the most salient *biological* fact about human beings is the size of our cerebral cortex and, hence, our capacity for learning, for self-reflection and for creativity in language, art and a host of other areas that together make up what, at any place and time, we label "culture."

*Crude* sociobiology theorizes a virtual one-to-one correspondence between certain supposedly gendered, supposedly survival-relevant behaviors (e.g., the male propensity for promiscuity and the female propensity for monogamy) and certain genetic patterns.

*Sophisticated* sociobiology argues (I believe correctly) that our most important genetic legacy is a flexible cerebral cortex that enables us to be the culture-creating, problem-solving, environmentally adaptive creatures that we are.

This does not mean that our behavior is infinitely malleable; some of it is bound by "critical periods" in our development (e.g., fluent language acquisition). Nor does it mean that genes and hormones count for nothing. What it does mean is that genetic and hormonal legacies flexibly interact with cognitive and social processes, with resulting cultural diversity – but not infinite diversity – in the way that our lives, including our sexual lives, are lived.

The behavior of other mammals is much more directly under genetic and hormonal control. That is why their sexual and aggressive behaviors correlate as well as they do with prenatal and postnatal hormonal events. In human beings, by contrast, "hormones do not rage; they insinuate."[9]

As a Christian social scientist, I have taken the time to

summarize this complicated interplay between nature, nurture and human freedom because it seems to me just what one would expect from the standpoint of biblical anthropology. If we are both "dust of the earth" and "made in the image of God" – called to accountable dominion and community, but within the bounds of our creatureliness – then we neither can ignore our bodily limits nor assume (when it suits our political purposes) that we simply are running on the biological or environmental equivalent of automatic pilot as regards our sexuality.

Our biology, which includes individual differences working within species-wide similarities, is like the needlework canvas on which we embroider the pattern of our lives. Some of us collect more (or different) colored threads than others with which to do this, but all of us – as we mature – have increasing control over how we will work the threads together onto the canvas. To claim either more or less freedom is disingenuous.

The interplay between nature, nurture and human freedom also helps explain something I expressed earlier – namely, that our Old Testament and New Testament ancestors were correct in treating various non-normative sexual acts as things to which anyone could be tempted. Despite the species-wide bias toward heterosexuality, any number of forces can influence people to engage in variations. That is why people are tempted to speak of the social construction of sexuality and to assume that every expression of it is equally possible, depending only on the requisite environmental reinforcers.

This again is a case of not taking biology seriously enough; yet, there is sufficient truth in the social constructionist hyperbole to make us sit up and take notice. Consider the example of the Sambian adolescent boys of New Guinea, who have a ritual period during which they engage older men in fellatio in order to acquire their virility, then go on to marry and lead heterosexual lives. Consider also the Latin American practice of a self-identified heterosexual having sex with another man, maintaining that he is not homosexual as long as he is the inserter and not the receiver of a penis.

Our biblical ancestors did not need to know the subtleties of the nature-nurture debate in order to observe that people could be tempted to various non-normative sexual activities. The real issue is not the origin of such behaviors, but the enduring reasons for their condemnation.

## Individual Fulfillment Revisited

Theological arguments for the acceptance of homosexual behavior, then, cannot get very far by appealing to biological determinism. Some advocates for gays have realized this and, thus, seek an alternative justification.

One biologist candidly admits that "most of the links in the chain of reasoning from biology to sexual orientation and public policy do not hold up under scrutiny." He then, however, goes on to assert that:

> [A]t the political level, a requirement that an unconventional trait be inborn or immutable is an inhumane criterion for a society to use in deciding which of its nonconformists it will grant tolerance. Even if homosexuality were entirely a matter of choice, attempts to extirpate it by social and criminal sanctions devalue basic human freedoms and diversity.[10]

Here the appeal is ethical, not biological; as a society we must, to be humane, promote "basic human freedoms and diversity." To the biologist just quoted, these criteria trump all others. And, of course, they do, if one accepts the modern liberal paradigm with little or no qualification – which means, among other things, that one assumes ethics can be done in a total biological vacuum and without looking too closely at what is required to make a society truly "humane."

Two recent attempts to develop this argument in the context of theological ethics are William Countryman's *Dirt, Greed, and Sex* and John Shelby Spong's *Living in Sin*.[11]

Countryman, for the most part, assiduously stays away from appeals to general revelation (as mediated by modern science) in his attempt to justify – or at least render morally neutral – sexual activities outside the bounds of heterosexual monogamy. Rather, he argues that biblical proscriptions against various sexual acts were expressions of ritual purity laws. These laws maintained boundaries between God's people and their pagan neighbors, and established male property rights over women and children in a collectivist society that subordinated individual fulfillment to a group identity based on bloodlines.

According to Countryman, however, the New Testament people of God no longer are chosen according to ethnic pedigree, and the New Testament calls for purity of heart, not body. That is why Gentiles were admitted to the church without circumcision or thebobservance of complex food laws. Church members with "weaker" consciences were free to continue observing such laws, and stronger, more enlightened members were not to scorn them for doing so. Nevertheless, the new norm was clear: "the equality of all human beings under grace and the priority of love over all other virtues."[12]

Moreover, Countryman argues, since biblical purity laws existed to preserve a collectivist society (rather than an individually-oriented one like our own), any attempt to enforce them – whether in regard to eating, excreting, birth, death or sexual activity – represents a denial of the dignity and autonomy of the individual. He accepts the modernist assumption that individual well-being requires freedom and self-determination in the context of interpersonal fulfillment, and a rejection of socially dictated relations.

Thus, each person "owns" his or her unique "sexual property" (i.e., degree and range of sexual expressiveness). One should exchange it not (as under the purity codes) for the "exterior goods" represented by material security and legitimate offspring, but for "interior" or psychological goods such as friendship, intimacy, comfort and counsel. Provided that such an exchange takes place within the deeper norm of "the equality of all human beings under grace and the priority of love," it matters almost not at all which organs are placed in what orifices of which organisms.

Thus, Countryman concludes:

> The gospel allows no rule against the following, in and of themselves: masturbation, nonvaginal heterosexual intercourse, bestiality, polygamy, homosexual acts, or erotic art and literature. The Christian [of "weaker conscience"] is free to be repelled by any or all of these and may continue to practice her or his own purity code in relation to them. What we are not free to do is impose our codes on others. Like all sexual acts, these may be genuinely wrong where they also involve an offense against the [sexual] property of another, denial of the equality of women and men, or an idolatrous substitution of sex for the reign of God as the goal of human existence.[13]

> The moral in all this is that the heterosexual majority in church and society – and particularly its male leaders – are in no position to hold self-identified gays to a higher standard of sexual conduct than they are willing to insist on for members of their own group.

When Countryman speaks of "the reign of God," as I understand it, he is speaking of a realized eschatology in which law (including the purity code to which it gave rise) is replaced by grace, and legalistic regulations give way to the larger, two-fold norm of loving God and loving a neighbor as oneself.

And although he cautions readers about the religious dangers of sexual idolatry, he clearly believes the larger religious problem is sexual prudery and inhibition, which he sees as regressive remnants of purity-law thinking, unconnected to either creation or the fall.

I will leave it to better trained theologians and biblical scholars to determine the merits of Countryman's eschatology and its tenuous connection to creation and sin. What I will say as a social scientist is that his utopian view of sex, constrained by little except "equality" and "love" (both notoriously elastic terms that can be used to justify anything and everything), is astonishingly naïve.

After all, the Sigmund Freud who wrote *The Future of an Illusion* (thereby demonstrating that he was no friend to organized religion)[14] was the same Freud who, three years later, wrote *Civilization and Its Discontents*. In that volume, he claimed that the control of sexual and aggressive urges – ideally through sublimation, rather than through the less-healthy routes of repression, denial, projection or reaction formation – was essential for civilization.

"Sublimation of instincts," he wrote, "is an especially conspicuous feature of cultural development: it is what makes it possible for higher psychical activities, scientific, artistic, or ideological, to play such an important part in civilized life."[15]

There is more than a touch of Western chauvinism in Freud's equation of sexual self-control with European civilization in the 1920s. The larger truth he was tapping into, however, is this: Whether we live in simple or complex cultures, our sexual and aggressive impulses are the "loose cannons" of our human nature. Sources of great energy, they are at the same time notoriously untrustworthy guides as to what is good for us in the long run, individually or collectively. That is why every enduring culture, simple or complex has been at pains to regulate them.

But, in our own culture, we live with the legacy of 30 years of largely unregulated sexual expression, practiced not just with the passive permission but also with the active encouragement of many mainline church leaders and scholars. The results make for very stark reading:

In 1992, AIDS became the leading killer of American men between the ages of 25 and 44, and the fourth highest among women in the same age range.

Between 1960 and 1990, the American divorce rate more than doubled, and we now can expect fully 40 percent of American children to experience the divorce of their parents.

Births outside of marriage went from five percent to almost 30 percent of all births and, among inner city African Americans, the rate now is 68 percent. Almost a million children are born out of wedlock annually, and a million and a half abortions are performed each year.

Adolescents become sexually active at ever earlier ages so that, by now, one in four 14-year-olds has experienced sexual intercourse.

Clearly, most of this sexual chaos cannot be blamed on self-identified gays. If anything, the main culprits are adult heterosexual males. It is fashionable today to focus on the "irresponsibility" of unmarried teenage mothers. For every five teenage mothers, however, there only are two teenage fathers because more than two-thirds of teenage mothers are impregnated by men over the age of 20.

Indeed, some 74 percent of young women who have had intercourse before the age of 14, and 60 percent of those who have done so before age 15, report having had sex against their will.

Adult heterosexual males also are responsible for most cases of sexual abuse, including rape, incest and child molestation. And while some of this abuse is inflicted on children by biological fathers, even more of it is by stepfathers, mothers' boyfriends and other unrelated males living in female-headed households. Given that almost 40 percent of American children now live apart from their biological fathers, the risk of such abuse is likely to escalate – absent a renewed campaign to fashion strong marriages characterized by responsibility, fidelity and mutual respect.

The moral in all this is that the heterosexual majority in church and society – and particularly its male leaders – is in no position to hold self-identified gays to a higher standard of sexual conduct than they are willing to insist on for members of their own group.

And while it no doubt is true that most male church leaders do not engage in the kind of irresponsible sexual practices listed above, they passively, if not actively, have been complicitous in their spread.

In the 1970s and 1980s, for example, most mainline Protestant denominations severely cut back funding to their national family ministries programs, while continuing to fund government lobbying efforts. Church leaders simply concluded that rising levels of teenage sexual activity, divorce, single parenthood and the feminization of poverty were inevitable and irreversible. Instead of calling everyone to higher standards of behavior, they lobbied for a combination of governmental and therapeutic programs to cushion the negative effects of these trends.

Sociologist David Blankenhorn observes that:

> [O]ver the past three decades, many religious leaders – especially in the mainline Protestant denominations – have largely abandoned marriage as a vital area of religious attention, essentially handing the entire matter over to opinion leaders and divorce lawyers in the secular society. Some members of the clergy seem to have lost interest in defending and strengthening marriage. Others report that they worry about offending members of their congregations who are divorced or unmarried ... [And when couples do] want to get married, many church leaders do little more than rent them the space and preside at the ceremony.[16]

Thus, the reigning sexual ethos in mainline Protestant churches, at best, has been a fatalistic resignation to current trends and, at worst, a romanticization of sexual freedom aided by dubious theologizing of the sort exemplified in Countryman's and Spong's work.

Moreover, in their haste to distance themselves from the sexual prudery and anxiety of parents, church leaders and

theologians largely have ignored one of the Bible's main reasons for calling us to sexual restraint – namely, God's concern for the vulnerable.

Countryman obviously is right that the Bible emerged
from a patriarchal and nationalistic culture in which men
dominated women and bloodlines represented the highest
human loyalty. Feminist exegetes equally are right to see the
occasional stories of powerful Old Testament women as a
foreshadowing of the New Testament breakdown of barriers
between Jew and Greek, slave and free, male and female.

What *neither* has acknowledged, however, is that the Old
Testament law also served – in contrast to norms in many
non-Israelite cultures – to curb or at least regulate patriarchal
practices:

> The extended family-clan-tribe system of ancient Israel,
> though undeniably patriarchal, provided an effective
> social welfare system for the vulnerable. Widows, single
> mothers, fatherless children and aliens were cared for
> within local communities. Modern individualism, with its
> reliance on the state to care for the needy, is neither as
> personal nor as efficient.[17]

Today's church needs to recover a high view of sexual discipline – not primarily to pander to ancient purity codes, but to
embody the enduring biblical norm of protecting the vulnerable and integrating them into the community. In the words of
Tim Stafford, a longtime specialist in youth ministry:

"Sexual chaos hurts everybody, but most of all it hurts the
poor and the weak. In the midst of chaos, the young, beautiful
and rich [whether straight or gay] will seem to thrive, at least
for a time. Vulnerable people – particularly children, women
and poor people – will suffer."

He also astutely observes that "no double standard of
morality between the suburbs and the ghetto is possible.
Underclass people are not going to listen to middle-class people preaching a message they don't live themselves. If chaotic
sexuality is a disaster in poor black society, you had better

admit it is a disaster in white society."[18]

## Some Advice to Both Sides in the Debate

I have not appealed, so far, to any of the arguments from creation to support the norm of heterosexual monogamy and celibate singleness. This is not because I do not accept such arguments, but because they have been made cogently enough by others with more exegetical expertise[19] and also because I believe the argument based on the need to protect vulnerable groups has been insufficiently appreciated in this debate.

But is it not the case that self-identified gays also are a vulnerable group? Have they not been closeted, forced to lead double lives, physically threatened, denied their civil rights and vilified by church and society alike? And is the church not thereby called to protect them as well?

The answer to the above questions obviously is yes. Before we decide how such protection should be structured, however, we need to remember that the concept of "constitutional" homosexual orientation arose when Victorian doctors shifted attention from individual homosexual *acts* to the concept of homosexuality as a *pervasive personality structure.* Thus, writes Michel Foucault:

> The nineteenth century homosexual became a personage, a past, a case history, and a childhood. ... Nothing that went into his total composition was unaffected by his sexuality. It was everywhere present in him: at the root of all his actions. ... The sodomite had been a temporary aberration; the homosexual was now a species.[20]

If Foucault is correct, then it is highly ironic that "the category Victorians invented to stigmatize homosexuality has now become the basis for celebrating it."[21]

Is continuing this essentialist line of thinking really in *anyone's* interests, especially when we recall the methodological difficulties of defining just what "threshold homosexuality" consists of, let alone what causes it? Might it not even be preferable to return to the language of our recent ancestors who, knowing nothing about theories of sexual orientation, concluded that some people simply were "not the marrying kind" and try to deal with each such case on a compassionate, individual basis that declines to make global, fatalistic attributions about sexual orientation?

At the other extreme, does anyone in the church seriously believe that, in the service of individual fulfillment, we theologically should underwrite almost any consensual sexual activity people choose to engage in, at whatever stage of their lives, for whatever reason?

I already have noted how such "Enlightenment individualism run wild" has affected the most vulnerable groups in our society. Is it the church's mission to continue rubber-stamping this naïve deference to sexual rights with only minimal responsibility? Or is the church called – in this area as in others – to be a counter-cultural community of mutual regard and service in which voluntary self-restraint, far from being an outdated legalism or the arbitrary demand of a capricious God, is an essential foundation for the secure inclusion and flourishing of everyone who confesses the name of Christ?

If the answer to the above question is yes, as I believe it is, this does not mean we must pretend (in Lewis Smedes' words) that we are "angels driving around in automobiles," dualistically denying the sexual signals of our bodies.[22] Sexual desire is very real and can have effects ranging from preoccupation to addiction, regardless of one's professed sexual orientation.

Whether self-identified as gay or straight, then, we need to bear one another's burdens without self-righteous condemnation. But we also must not let each other be tempted to the cheap grace represented by the doctrine of unfettered self-fulfillment. That path eventually leads not only to the victimization of others, but also – a tragic irony – to the depletion of the very self one is so desperately trying to fulfill.

Thus, as Richard Hay's AIDS-stricken friend Gary put it

on the threshold of his own death:

"Are homosexuals to be excluded from the community of faith? Certainly not. But anyone who joins such a community should know that it is a place of transformation, of discipline, of learning, and not merely a place to be comforted or indulged."[23]

For the record (and here I speak personally rather than professionally), I believe primary homosexuals do exist – that is, people with a consistent and longstanding pattern of attraction directed exclusively to members of their own sex.

But we should note that the percentage of such people in the general population (as opposed to the percentage converging in a few large cities) is small. Only 2.7 percent of adult men and 0.8 percent of women in the *Sex in America* study had exclusively same-sex sexual contacts within the past year. That does not mean their concerns should be ignored, but it ought to keep us from making exaggerated claims based on faulty assumptions about the prevalence of homosexuality. Conservatives should be less inclined toward hysteria about the safety of their children and the imminence of a "gay takeover" of various institutions since primary homosexuality is rare and neither casually acquired nor easily discarded. And liberals should be less inclined toward zealous advocacy for gay empowerment, if this means going beyond the support of civil rights, freedom from harassment, and pastoral and practical care for people with AIDS, to devoting disproportionate attention to a relatively small group.

We have our work cut out for us dealing with other critical issues: the continuing fallout of divorce, single parenthood and various forms of sexual libertarianism indulged in by non-gays.

There is a final reason for urging caution on the question of ordaining gays and blessing their unions: namely, the fact that gays themselves are divided on these issues, although the public stage still is largely held by advocates of the rhetoric of individual fulfillment.

As a charter member of the second wave of feminism, I am sympathetic when marginalized groups are reluctant to air internal differences in public for fear of being divided, conquered, and sent back to theirrespective closets. But I also believe it is a mark of maturity when legitimate, publicly-aired differences within a social movement begin to replace the requirement of lock-step adherence to a single party line. This now is happening with greater regularity among feminists and I hope to see something similar from gays, for only then will we be able to pose better questions and arrive at better answers.

My point simply is that I have heard enough unnuanced arguments between gay advocates and their adversaries. I want to hear strenuous public debate *among gays themselves* – particularly those who identify themselves as Christians – about their own internal differences.

And here is what I hope eventually will emerge from such a debate: just as mature Christian feminists should admit that male sexism is not the original sin and women are not the pristine, new creation, so self-identified homosexuals must come to admit that heterosexism is not the original sin and gays and lesbians are not the new creation. That kind of naïve triumphalism is understandable in the early stages of a movement to unite people who have been misunderstood and victimized in the past. It ultimately, however, is inappropriate among Christians who recognize that the original sin still is what it always was – namely, the desire of all human beings to deal with God strictly on their own terms and to worship whatever part of the creation they happen to want to elevate to the position of the creator. In this inherent weakness, we all are fellow travelers and our fallenness wreaks havoc on us all.

*Mary Stewart Van Leeuwen is professor of psychology and*

*philosophy at Eastern College, St. David's, Pa., and resident scholar at its Hestenes Center for Christian Women in Leadership. Her research interests include social and cross-cultural psychology, gender studies, philosophy of social science and practical theology. This article first appeared in* Interpretation, *April 1997 and is reprinted with permission*

## Endnotes

1.  C. P. Snow, *The Two Cultures and a Second Look* (London: Cambridge University Press, 1964) 9.

2.  Robert T. Michael, John H. Gagnon, Edward O. Laumann, and Gina Kolata, *Sex in America: A Definitive Survey* (Boston: Little, Brown, 1994). A more detailed and academic version of the same study can be found in Edward O. Laumann, John H. Gagnon, Robert T. Michael and Stuart Michaels, *The Social Organization of Sexuality* (University of Chicago Press, 1994). For establishing accurate prevalence rates of anything, *only* random-sample studies are adequate – which is why earlier, non-random surveys, such as the ones done by Alfred Kinsey in the 1940s, are unreliable indicators of the prevalence of homosexuality.

3.  Michael et al., *Sex in America*, 183. These researchers are right to remind readers that male and female homosexuality, however one defines the term, yields rather different historical, behavioral and psychological profiles. Moreover, biological mechanisms that have been proposed to explain male homosexuality often cannot be generalized to women. Since research and funding for causal studies of homosexuality have generally concentrated on males and ignored females (nothing new in the world of science), this incongruity goes largely unremarked in the media.

4.  Heather Looy, "Born Gay? A Critical Review of Biological Research on Homosexuality," *Journal of Psychology and Christianity* 14, no. 3 (1995) 194-214 (198-99). See also Janet Shibley Hyde, *Understanding Human Sexuality*, 5th ed. (New York: McGraw-Hill, 1994) Ch. 15-16.

5.  Simon LeVay, "A Difference in Hypothalamic Structure Between Heterosexual and Homosexual Men," *Science* 253 (1991) 1034-37.

6. J. M. Bailey and R. C. Pillard, "A Genetic Study of Male Sexual Orientation," *Archives of General Psychiatry* 48 (1991) 1089-96.

7. D. H. Hamer, S. Hu, V. L. Magnuson, N. Hu and A. M. Pattatuci, "A Linkage Between DNA Markers on the X Chromosome and Male Sexual Orientation." *Science* 261 (1993) 321-27.

8. See Looy ("Born Gay?") for a more thorough and very accessible review of the literature in all three areas.

9. Louise Lander, *Images of Bleeding: Menstruation as Ideology* (New York: Orlando, 1988) 162.

10. William Byne, "The Biological Evidence Challenged," *Scientific American* 270:5 (May 1994) 50.

11. John Shelby Spong, *Living in Sin: A Bishop Rethinks Human Sexuality* (New York: HarperCollins, 1988); L. William Countryman, *Dirt, Greed, and Sex: Sexual Ethics in the New Testament and Their Implications for Today* (Philadelphia: Fortress, 1988). My critique here will be limited to Countryman's work.

12. Countryman, *Dirt, Greed, and Sex*, 241.

13. *Ibid.*, 243-44.

14. Sigmund Freud, *The Future of an Illusion* (New York: Norton, 1961; orig. 1927).

15. Sigmund Freud, *Civilization and its Discontents* (New York: Norton, 1961; orig. 1930) 49.

16. David Blankenhorn, *Fatherless America: Confronting Our Most Urgent Social Problem* (New York: Basic Books, 1995) 231.

17. Mardi Keyes, *Feminism and the Bible* (Downers Grove: Inter-Varsity, 1995) 8.

18. Tim Stafford, *Sexual Chaos* (Downers Grove: Intervarsity, 1993) 26-27.

19. See, for example, David Atkinson, *Homosexuals in the Christain Fellowship* (Grand Rapids: Eerdmans, 1979); Richard Hays, "Relations Natural and Unnatural: A Response to John Boswell's Exegesis of Romans 1," *JRE* 14 (1984) 184-215. See also the report of the Committee to Study Homosexuality,

*Acts of Synod of the Christian Reformed Church in North America* (Grand Rapids: C.R.C. Board of Publications, 1973) 609-33, and Tom Schmidt, *Straight and Narrow? Compassion and Clarity in the Homosexuality Debate* (Downers Grove: InterVarsity, 1995).

20. Michel Foucault, *The History of Sexuality*, trans. Robert Hurley (New York: Random House, 1978) 43.

21. Stafford, *Sexual Chaos*, 131.

22. Lewis Smedes, *Sex for Christians* (Grand Rapids: Eerdmans, 1976).

23. Richard Hays, "Awaiting the Redemption of Our Bodies," *Sojourners* 20, no. 6 (July 1991) 20-21.

CHAPTER 2

# Homosexuality and
# the Christian Sex Ethic

### Stanley J. Grenz

*D*espite any outside influences, the biblical
writers were imbued with the narratives of
God, acting in human history, that lay at the
foundation of the Hebrew and early Christian faith
communities. Consequently, the scriptural injunctions
against homosexual practices as "unnatural" derived
fundamentally from an outlook toward God's intention
for human life as depicted in the biblical narrative. The
"natural" is what is in accordance with God's purpose
for human existence. And divine purposes encompass
human sexual practice.*

In October 1996, Christian leaders from across Canada
gathered in Toronto for the gala World Shapers '96 confer-
ence sponsored by the Evangelical Fellowship of Canada.
While the thousand conferees were putting the final touches
on the opening night festivities – heartily singing "Bind Us
Together" – members of the Word of Life Church in nearby
St. Catherine's broke the unanimity of the event by scattering
about pamphlets critical of the EFC. EFC's flagship journal,
*Faith Today*, had just published an essay on human sexuality

that Word of Life's pastor, Peter Youngren, claimed denied the power of the gospel to deliver homosexuals from their "sinful, God-dishonoring condition."

Barely a year later, a group of concerned citizens (including several conservative Christians) sought to hold an open-air public informational forum in downtown Vancouver to focus on the inappropriateness of using certain literature on homosexuality in the public schools.

The meeting, however, never got off the ground. A cadre of shouting gay and lesbian activists took control of the microphones and intimidated would-be attendees, while law enforcement officers stood idly by.

These two events – instigated by people whom we might dismiss as occupying opposite fringes of the political spectrum – stand as reminders of just how emotionally charged and potentially divisive the issue of homosexuality has become – not only in North American society, but also within the church.

> Human sexuality – understood as the quest to forsake our solitude through relations with others – finds ultimate fulfillment through participation in the community of believers who enjoy fellowship with God through Christ.

Conservative Christians believe the Bible speaks clearly to this issue, and they note that, throughout its history, the church consistently and unequivocally has opposed homosexual behavior. But why?

In what follows, I seek to answer this question. My intent is to go beneath the strictures themselves and draw out from the foundational biblical narrative the ethical stance that motivated biblical writers – including Paul and the compiler(s) of the Holiness Code – to declare same-sex intercourse "unnatural" and, thus, unethical.

My assumption is that, despite any influence other sources had on them, these authors were imbued with the narratives of God, acting in human history, that lay at the foundation of the Hebrew and early Christian faith communities.

Consequently, the scriptural injunctions against homosexual practices were embedded in a teleological understanding of the "natural." This understanding derived fundamentally from an outlook toward God's intention for human life as depicted in the biblical narrative. For the biblical writers, then, the "natural" is what is in accordance with God's *telos* (purpose) for human existence. And divine purposes encompass human sexual practice.

In keeping with this assumption, I begin the discussion by placing human sexuality in the context of the biblical narrative. My goal in this first section is to set forth in summary fashion a Christian theological understanding of sexuality and marriage.

The theological understanding of sexuality that emerges from these reflections, in turn, provides the foundation for an ethical appraisal of same-sex intercourse.

Then, I next interact with the question of sin as it relates to same-sex intercourse and homosexuality in general.

Finally, I round out the discussion with a few comments about homosexuality and sexual expression.

In this manner, I develop a basically teleological approach to the contemporary issue, an approach that draws from considerations of God's *telos* for human relationships[1] as given, in part, in the creation narratives.

## Human Sexuality in Theological Perspective

An awareness of human sexual distinctions appears almost immediately in the biblical story. Standing at the apex of the first creation narrative is God's fashioning of humankind in the divine image as male and female (Gen. 1:27-28).

Sexual differentiation is even more prominent in the second creation story, which focuses on God's creation of the woman to deliver the man from his solitude (Gen. 2:18-24).

Throughout the Bible, the creation stories play an ongoing role, even in texts that emerged within different social contexts. Paul, for example, appealed to the Genesis narratives, even though he lived in the more urban, less agrarian culture of the first century Roman Empire.

Thus, the creation of humankind as male and female is central to the understanding of human sexuality found throughout the entire biblical story. This broader creation-based understanding lies behind the biblical injunctions that depict homosexual intercourse as "unnatural" and, hence, unethical.

## The Nature of Human Sexuality

Human beings are sexual creatures. But what is the significance of our sexuality?[2]

One answer, according to the biblical narrative, is procreation. Procreation is a crucial aspect of our creation as male and female, especially after the fall (e.g., Gen. 4:1). Yet, the begetting of children is not the only purpose for our creation as both male and female.

The second creation story suggests that our sexuality is not limited to the physical characteristics and activities associated with male and female reproductive roles. Sexuality encompasses our fundamental existence in the world as embodied people. It includes our way of being in and relating to the world. Above all, however, sexuality represents our incompleteness as embodied creatures. Hence, sexuality lies behind the human quest for completeness. This yearning for wholeness, which we express through our seemingly innate drive to bond with others, forms an important basis for the interpersonal dimension of existence.

This Genesis narrative highlights the interpersonal aspect of human sexuality. The story presents the creation of the woman as God's solution to Adam's solitude. The man enjoyed a relationship with the animals; yet none of them could provide what he truly needed – a partner with whom he could bond. Cognizant of this situation, God created another – the woman – to deliver Adam from his isolation. The man greeted her with the joyous declaration: She is "bone of my bones and flesh of my flesh" (Gen. 2:23). The episode concludes with the narrator's application to the phenomenon of male-female bonding: "For this reason a man will leave his father and mother and be united to his wife, and they will become one flesh" (v. 24). In this manner, the narrator points out that the drive toward bonding finds expression in the coming together of male and female in the unity of people we know as marriage.

The interpersonal dynamic, however, is not limited to the sexual bond. Our creation as male and female also contributes to personal identity development. We discover – or construct – who we are in our embodied maleness or femaleness partly through our interactions with the other sex.

This dimension of our sexuality also is evident in the second creation account. Adam first sensed his own maleness when confronted with the woman. That encounter led him to declare joyfully, "She shall be called 'woman,' for she was taken out of man" (Gen. 2:23 NIV). In a sense, this aspect of the story provides an explanation of the first narrative, which links the *imago dei* to our creation as male and female (Gen. 2:27). We discover God's intention for us to be the divine image bearers – and, hence, discover our full humanness – through our interaction with one another as male and female. This can occur within marriage, of course, but it also is operative in all male-female relationships.

The Old Testament narrative views the sexual bond between husband and wife as the foundation for human social relationships – family, tribe and, eventually, nation. Jesus, however, inaugurated one significant alteration to this pattern. Rather than elevating earthly ancestry, he looked to his heavenly parentage, counting as his true family "whoever does the will of my Father in heaven" (Matt. 12:50). In keeping with his own example, Jesus challenged his followers to place their relationship to him above all familial ties (Matt. 10:37). And he promised them a new spiritual family to compensate for the loss that discipleship would exact from them (Mark 10:29-30).

According to Jesus, the primary human bond is not marriage and family, as important as these are, but the company of disciples. In this manner, human sexuality – understood as the quest to forsake our solitude through relations with others – finds ultimate fulfillment through participation in the community of believers who enjoy fellowship with God through Christ. And our innate incompleteness, related as it is to our fundamental sexuality, points toward the consummation of God's activity in the community of God's eternal kingdom.

En route to that future day, humans enter into a variety of personal relationships. Most of these are informal and somewhat fluid. Others are permanent and exclusive. Although both are the outworking of the human drive toward bonding and, hence, in this sense are "sexual," they differ widely, including with respect to the type of sexual behavior proper to each.

In this manner, the biblical narrative provides the foundation for a rich understanding of human sexuality that forms a stark contrast to what the Dutch gay theologian, Pim Pronk, bemoans as the modern "static-mechanical" model.

The model Pronk critiques treats human behavior as divisible into autonomous parts, among which is sexual activity. It draws a sharp distinction between sexual and non-sexual behavior on the basis of whether or not the sex organs are involved. And it views the link between the sex drive and sexual behavior somewhat like the connection between "the wound-up alarm clock and its going off."[3]

Pronk concludes that this static-mechanical view suffers from a "one-sided accent on the *private* character of sexual relations" and, as a result, it "fails to do justice to the social dimension" of human sexuality.[4]

## Sexuality and Marriage

Historically, the most significant social expression of human sexuality is marriage. Viewed from the perspective of the Bible, marriage entails the coming together of male and female to form an exclusive sexual bond. The biblical writers connect this human relationship with procreation and child-rearing, as well as a focal point for companionship as husband and wife share intimacy and friendship.

Marriage carries another crucial meaning in Scripture: It provides a metaphor of spiritual truth. The bond uniting husband and wife symbolizes certain aspects of the relation between God and God's people.

The Old Testament prophets found in marriage an appropriate vehicle for telling the story of Yahweh's faithfulness in the face of Israel's idolatry.

> The dynamic of love involved in friendship is generally not contained within exclusive boundaries. For this reason, friendship reflects the open, non-exclusive, expanding aspect of God's love – the divine love that seeks to include within the circle of fellowship those still outside its boundaries.

The New Testament authors drew from this Old Testament imagery (e.g., Rom. 9:25; I Peter 2:9-10). They spoke of marriage as a picture of the great mystery of salvation – the union of Christ and the Church. Marriage illustrates Christ's self-sacrifice for the Church, as well as submission to Christ (Eph. 5:21-33) by people who anticipate the future coming of their Lord (Matt. 25:1-13; Rev. 19:7; 21:9-10; 21:2).

In this manner, marriage provides a picture of the exclusive nature of our relationship to God in Christ. Just as marriage is to be an exclusive, inviolate and, hence, holy bond, so also our relationship to God must be exclusive and holy for, as God's covenant people, we can serve no other gods but the one God (Ex. 20:3). By extension, the exclusive love shared by husband and wife reflects the holiness of the divine love present within the triune God, which then overflows from God to creation.

The ancient Hebrews clearly viewed marriage as normative. The New Testament, however, opened the way for believers to fulfill a divine vocation as single people, evidenced by John the Baptist, Jesus and Paul. This dimension of the biblical narrative reminds us that ,whether married or single, we all enter into a variety of informal relationships and friendships with others. These friendships need not be permanent, they rarely are exclusive (that is, limited to only two people), and they seldom are entered through formal covenant.

Relationships between single people provide the clearest example of a non-exclusive, non-marital friendship bond. Like marriage, friendship carries theological meaning. In contrast to the marital union, the informal friendship bond is less defined and, therefore, more open to the inclusion of others. Further, the dynamic of love involved in friendship generally is not contained within exclusive boundaries. For this reason, friendship reflects the open, non-exclusive, expanding aspect of God's love – the divine love that seeks to include within the circle of fellowship those still outside its boundaries.

## Sexuality and the Sex Act

As several contemporary philosophers have pointed out, events are more than physical happenings because every event always occurs within a context that contributes to its meaning. Similarly, the meaning of a human act is dependent not only on the act itself, but also on the context in which it transpires, which includes the actor's intent.[5]

As a human act, sexual intercourse is more than a physical

occurrence. It is a highly meaningful metaphor. But the meaning of any act of sexual intercourse is dependent both on the physical act itself and the context in which it occurs. The participants pour meaning into the act by the intent that motivates them and by the relationship they bring to it.

The Christian ethic is based on the belief that God intends the sex act to carry specific meanings. Sexual intercourse is not valuable primarily as a means to some other goal, including such good purposes as pleasure or pregnancy. Rather, the sex act is what Roman Catholic ethicist James Hanigan calls a symbolic or ritual activity. He writes, "Sex, then, finds its proper value as an act which focuses, celebrates, expresses and enhances the meaning of our substantive activities and relationships."[6]

In part, we may view sexual intercourse as the ritual that celebrates committed, loving relationships. Yet, each of us enjoys many such relationships, which we celebrate in various non-genital ways. In fact, sexual intercourse would deeply wound, if not completely destroy, most of these relationships. Consequently, the context in which the sex act occurs is crucial, so much so that in certain contexts the sex act simply is inappropriate. According to the biblical writers, the divinely-intended meanings of the sex act emerge only when the act occurs within one specific context – marriage.

Practiced within marriage as the sign of the unconditional, covenantal love of husband and wife, sexual intercourse carries several important meanings. It is a beautiful symbol of the exclusive bond between the marriage partners, through which wife and husband reaffirm their commitment to each other. Further, it is a beautiful celebration of the mutuality of the relationship, as each partner reaffirms his or her desire to give pleasure to the other. And, because of its connection to procreation, the sex act expresses the openness of husband and wife to the new life that may arise from their bond.

Because of the meanings the sex act is intended to carry, the marital bond provides the sole proper context for sexual intercourse. The Old Testament law codified this view (e.g., Ex. 20:14), and Jesus and the New Testament apostles reaffirmed it (e.g., Matt. 19:3-9; I Cor. 6:9).

As a result, the traditional Christian sex ethic rightly advocates chastity in the form of abstinence in singleness and fidelity in marriage. This ethic, in turn, provides the foundation for a Christian stance toward homosexuality.

## Christian Sex Ethic and Same-Sex Intercourse

Most participants in the contemporary discussion agree that certain homosexual practices – like certain heterosexual practices – are morally wrong. Lists of immoral behaviors commonly include such abuses as prostitution, rape and pederasty. But does this ethical judgment extend to all homosexual acts? More specifically, is same-sex intercourse morally wrong even when practiced within the context of a loving gay or lesbian relationship?

In dealing with this question, I will avoid the pattern of some advocates of the traditional position who enumerate the purported harmful physical or psychological effects of involvement in various homosexual behaviors.[7] Nor will I deal with the reciprocal argument of those who claim that homosexual liaisons must be affirmed simply because "they harm no one."[8]

I want to probe the ethics of same-sex intercourse viewed apart from any "side effects" it may or may not have. My goal here is to determine in what sense the act may be deemed unethical in and of itself. What is it about this practice that makes it morally suspect even when it occurs within the context of a stable homosexual relationship?

### Same-Sex Intercourse as a Deficient Act

As previously stated, the significance of any act arises in part from the context in which it occurs. Similarly, the physical act is important as an appropriate carrier of intended meaning: To serve as an authentic ritual, a physical act must have the capacity to symbolize the reality it ritualizes.[9] Viewed from this perspective, same-sex intercourse is deficient as a vehicle for conveying the intended meaning of the sex act. Because it ritually cannot enact the reality it symbolizes, it fails to make that reality present.

According to the biblical understanding, sexual intercourse involves the coming together of two people as sexual beings in a one-flesh union. It represents the act of two becoming one at the deepest level of their being (e.g., Gen. 2:23-24; Matt. 19:4-6).

As a result, the sex act entails more than the experience of sexual climax. (Indeed, sexual climax can occur apart from sexual intercourse.)

More crucial than the ability to attain sexual climax is the capability of the sex act to symbolize the uniting of two sexual people into one. As a ritual act, sexual intercourse must be able to represent physically (and, thus, make present) the two-in-one sexual bond it symbolizes.

This meaning readily is expressed in sexual relations between a man and a woman. Each engages in the sex act through the whole body, of course, but primarily through those body parts (vagina and penis) that most explicitly symbolize their existence as embodied, sexual beings; that most explicitly separate male from female; and that most readily allow male and female to complement each other. In this manner, both their own personal identities and their "otherness" or difference from each other as sexual creatures become the foundation for the expression of the bond they share. As a result, the sex act itself serves as a ritual act, an appropriate symbol of the union of two who are sexually "other" into a sexual bond.

It is not surprising that male-female intercourse provides such a vivid symbol of the sexual bond. As James Hanigan observes, "The unity ritualized and enacted in sexual behavior is a two-in-one flesh unity, a unity that has its created basis in the physical and biological complementarity of male and female."[10]

The partners in same-sex intercourse also bring to the act the physical features that most deeply represent their existence as sexual beings. But in this act, the specific body part each contributes to the act does not represent what distinguishes them from each other. Nor does it represent the unique contribution each brings to their sexual union because their roles in the act can be interchanged.

Further, in same-sex intercourse, some other body part (finger or artificial penis in lesbian acts, mouth or anus in male homosexual acts) routinely substitutes for the sexual organ that neither partner can provide. But whenever this occurs, one or the other partner presses an aspect of his or her anatomy into the service of the sex act that, because it is not the definitive mark of the person as a sexual being, is not normally viewed as sexual.

> As the biblical writers themselves suggest, the exclusive bond of husband and wife forms a fitting metaphor of the exclusivity of the divine-human relationship. The sex act, in turn, is the ritual celebration of this exclusive bond.

In this manner, same-sex intercourse loses the symbolic dimension of two-becoming-one that is present in male-female sex. At best, it only is a simulation of the two-becoming-one ritual that the act of sexual intercourse is designed to be. And a homosexual couple only can imitate the unity of two people joining together as sexual "others," so vividly symbolized in male-female coitus.

Hence, Hanigan is correct in concluding that homosexual acts ultimately are "only pretense or imaginative simulations of the real thing."[11]

## Sexual Intercourse Within the Wrong Context

If acts derive their meaning from the context in which they

occur, then same-sex intercourse also is deficient because it occurs within an improper context. That is, the context in which it is practiced – even if it is a stable gay or lesbian relationship – does not confirm the intended meaning of the sex act.

To understand this, we must return to the three meanings of the sex act within the context of marriage. At first glance, it would appear that when practiced in the context of a stable, monogamous homosexual relationship, same-sex intercourse could carry at least two of these meanings. The act conceivably could mark the celebration of the lifelong commitment of the two partners to each other, as well as the mutuality of their relationship.

Less possible, obviously, is the third meaning. Because children simply are not procreated in this manner, same-sex intercourse cannot express the openness of the couple to new life arising from their bond. At best, the act serves as an imitation of male-female procreative intercourse.

Are we to conclude, then, that ultimately the only basis on which same-sex intercourse can be discounted is its lack of procreative potential?

No. We drew from the biblical narrative the idea that the sex act is the ritual celebration of the exclusive bond of two people united in a one-flesh union. And we concluded that, when viewed from the biblical perspective, the marriage of male and female is the only appropriate expression of that exclusive sexual bond. Of course, this conclusion rules same-sex sexual bonding out of court, even when it involves a mutual, lifelong commitment.

But why privilege heterosexual marriage? Why set up the male-female sexual bond as the standard? Why could we not view same-sex intercourse as the expression of the bond uniting two people of the same sex, analogous to heterosexual intercourse as the ritual sexual act in marriage?

One response arises from another consideration drawn from the physical aspect of the sex act itself. It is instructive to note that, by its very nature, any specific occurrence of male-female sexual intercourse involves – and only can involve – two people, a male and a female. This characteristic forges a close link between the sex act and the reality it ritualizes because the sex act provides a vivid symbolic declaration of the monogamous nature of the biblical ideal for marriage. It also connects the sex act as a symbol with the begetting of children for, biologically, a child is the union of the contributions of two people – the biological father and the biological mother.

At this point, however, same-sex intercourse fundamentally differs from heterosexual intercourse. There is nothing inherent in this physical act that would limit involvement to two people. This observation leads us to ask: On what ritual basis would any homosexual bond necessarily consist of two and only two? If there is no intrinsic aspect of the ritual act that limits its participants to two, why should anyone privilege "monogamous" homosexual relations?

Further, if nothing intrinsic to the act inherently symbolizes the reality of two-becoming-one, then same-sex intercourse – even when practiced within a stable homosexual relationship – simply is unable to ritualize exclusivity. In contrast to heterosexual intercourse, it cannot function as the celebration of an exclusive bond and, therefore, cannot point to the exclusivity of the relationship God desires to have with us. In this way, same-sex intercourse loses the spiritual meaning of the sex act.

The same conclusion arises from a consideration of the nature of the bond being celebrated in the sex act. When viewed from the perspective we outlined earlier, same-sex intercourse entails a confusing of the bond of informal friendship with the male-female sexual bond of marriage.

We already noted that the otherness of the marital relationship is crucial to its symbolic significance. As Max Stackhouse declared, "the marriage bond is a community of love between those who are 'other.' This means not simply 'another' person, but one who is truly 'other.'"[12] Just as homosexual people cannot ritualize a two-become-one unity in the act of intercourse, so also they cannot become a two-become-one unity in the shared life of unity and difference that typifies the marriage of male and female.[13]

Stackhouse reminds us of one reason why this is crucial:

The marriage of a man to a woman ... remains the normative physical, social, and moral sign that we are not meant to be isolated individuals or to focus only on relationships with those who are already much like us. We are created for community with the Divine Other and with the human other, and the bonding of sexual otherness is the immediate and obvious evidence of this.[14]

Similarly, psychologist Ruth Tiffany Barnhouse appeals to the Song of Songs in declaring that "sexuality itself is a symbol of wholeness, of the reconciliation of opposites, of the loving at-one-ment between God and Creation."[15]

> Because of our depravity, we find at work within us desires, impulses and urges we did not consciously choose but which, instead, feel quite normal. Yet, we dare not entrust ourselves to our natural inclinations for these are not a sure guide to proper conduct.

These statements lead us back to the central significance of marriage that we noted earlier; namely, its theological symbolism. As the biblical writers themselves suggest, the exclusive bond of husband and wife forms a fitting metaphor of the exclusivity of the divine-human relationship. The sex act, in turn, is the ritual celebration of this exclusive bond. A homosexual relationship is not an appropriate context for the sex act because, in the context of such a relationship, sexual intercourse simply cannot express this intended meaning.

This is evident when we realize that every stable same-sex relation is, in fact, an informal bond between or among friends. As we noted earlier, the friendship bond ought not to find ritualized expression in a sexual act. Several considerations point out why this is so.

First, although like marriage friendship includes unity and difference, the difference exemplified between or among friends is not a sexual difference; same-sex friends do not manifest unity and difference sexually.[16]

Further, friendships can wither and die without necessarily incurring moral fault on the part of any of the friends. Although in marriage both friendship and sexual attraction can and do die, the biblical writers suggest that the severing of the marital relationship itself always involves moral fault, however hard it might be to pinpoint that fault.

Finally, friendship – which generally is neither an exclusive nor a formalized bond – proclaims the inclusive, rather than the exclusive, love of God. The intent of the sex act, however, is to celebrate exclusivity, not inclusivity.

Same-sex intercourse, then, introduces into the friendship bond the language of exclusivity and permanence that properly belongs solely to marriage. Of course, we could back away from the grammar of pair-bonding and conclude that same-sex intercourse intends to say nothing more than "I find you attractive." But mutual attraction never is a sufficient basis for sexual intimacy, regardless of the sexual preference of the people involved. As ethicist Edward Batchelor pointed out, "love does not always justify sexual union." The implication for homosexual attraction follows: "It is every bit as likely that the love of man for man or woman for woman bids them refrain from sexual intercourse as that it urges them to it."[17]

## The Christian Ethic and Homosexuality

I have looked at the implications of a Christian theology of sexuality for same-sex intercourse. In this process, I drew from the divine *telos* for human sexual relationships as indicated in the foundational stories of Genesis and reiterated in the New Testament to indicate why the sex act properly cannot occur within a homosexual relationship. In this sense, same-sex intercourse is "unnatural."

What does all this have to say about the contemporary phenomenon of homosexuality understood as a stable sexual orientation or preference? Specifically, in what sense, if any, is homosexuality sinful?

En route to an answer, I will look at the contemporary argument favoring a positive outlook toward homosexuality as a sexual "inversion." Only then can I seek to chart an alternative.

## The 'Naturalness' of Homosexuality

Many proponents of a more open stance view homosexuality as a stable sexual preference, which properly finds expression in acts such as same-sex intercourse. In effect, the apologetic for this position turns the biblical condemnation of homosexual behavior on its head. In contrast to Paul and others who claim that same-sex acts are "against nature," proponents assert that homosexuality, in fact, is "natural."

By "natural," some theorists mean nothing more than homosexuality is a naturally occurring phenomenon among humans. The central foundation for this approach is its purported presence in a variety of societies throughout history.

This approach, however, has been exploded by social constructivists such as David Greenberg,[18] who point out that homosexuality is not a single, identifiable, transcultural human condition. Instead, understandings of same-sex practices vary from culture to culture. These range from the ritualized rites of passage associated with adolescent sexual development found in several tribal societies[19] to the spiritualized pederasty of certain Greek philosophers, who downplayed any actual physical content within such relationships.[20]

Other proponents speak of the naturalness of homosexual preference in more individualistic terms. Homosexuality is natural, they assert, in that it is not the product of conscious personal choice. Rather than choosing their sexual orientation, this argument purports, gays and lesbians "discover" their homosexuality as a pre-existing reality. As Christian gay activist and writer Chris Glaser declared, "In my experience, sexual orientation was a given, like race or gender. How I responded in faith to that given was what was spiritually significant to me."[21] Christiane Gudorf draws out the erroneous, but commonly asserted, ethical implication:

> The agreement within medical and social science that sexual orientation is not chosen but more commonly discovered absolves homosexual orientation of sinfulness, and calls into question ... the unnaturalness of homosexual acts for those with homosexual orientation.[22]

Statements such as these are an important reminder that most people do not consciously set out to develop a specific sexual preference. At the same time, claims about its unchosen nature often harbor an overly simplistic picture of the development of homosexuality.

> Our calling is to exhibit in our relationships in the here and now God's intentions for human existence, which will be present in their fullness only in the future new community.

While the jury still is out on what causes any specific instance, most scientists and psychologists agree that a constellation of factors – biological predispositions, personal experiences and the attitudes and actions of others (including parents) – can contribute to disposing a person toward same-sex preference.

To this list we ought to add the constellation of social identities and roles that social constructionists like Greenberg declare are involved in the construction of homosexuality. Yet, in this equation, we dare not overlook the likelihood of some element of personal choice. Certain psychologists conclude that homosexuality is a pattern that develops over time and this conclusion opens the possibly of a limited, yet nevertheless active role, of the person himself or herself. In short, as the designation itself suggests, one's sexual orientation also is in some sense his or her sexual "preference," even if once set that preference "can hardly be abolished by an arbitrary act of will," to cite Greenberg's assessment.[23]

More important, however, is the ethical critique of this perspective. Ethicists remind us that to argue from any supposed natural reality to moral rectitude is to commit the "naturalistic fallacy;" that is, to deduce an "ought" from an "is." Ethics, however, is not the condoning of what is natural. Thus, even if homosexuality were indisputably "natural" for certain people, this would not in and of itself justify their engaging in same-sex practices.

Christian ethics takes this critique an additional step: In contrast to those who assert that no one can be held responsible for acting according to his or her nature, the Christian tradition declares that personal responsibility is not limited to matters in which we have full personal choice.

Why not? This question leads to the concept of sin. Viewed from the biblical perspective, sin means "missing the mark;" that is, failing to live up to God's intention for our lives. Rather than a somewhat localized debilitation, this failure can be felt in all areas of human existence and its presence predates our conscious choices. This, in part, is what the Reformers meant by "depravity."

Because of our depravity, we find at work within us desires, impulses and urges we did not consciously choose but which, instead, feel quite normal. Yet, we dare not entrust ourselves to our natural inclinations for these are not a sure guide to proper conduct. Jesus himself declared that evil deeds proceed from the human heart (Mark 7:21). Consequently, he instructed his disciples to distrust what they may perceive to be their natural inclinations and follow a radically new ethic.

Caution is necessary as much in our sexual conduct as in any aspect of life. The supposed naturalness of a person's same-sex preference does not set aside the biblical call to engage in genital sexual expression exclusively within monogamous heterosexual marriage. To assert otherwise, once again, is to commit the "naturalistic fallacy" of arguing from "what is" to "what ought to be."[24] The same fallacy would be at work if I were to set aside the biblical call to marital fidelity on the basis of the claim that, as a male, I naturally am promiscuous, as contemporary sociobiology suggests.

Rather than excusing us on the basis of the sensed natural-ness of our inclinations, the Bible offers divine grace in the midst of the realities of life. This grace brings both forgive-ness of our trespasses and power to overcome the workings of our human fallenness in the concrete situations we face.

This cautionary stance toward the appeal to what is natural must be tempered, however, by one additional consideration. Christian ethics does derive an "ought" from an "is";[25] an "is" does determine the Christian moral imperative. But this "is" ultimately is neither what once was, nor what now is. Instead, it is a future "is" – a "will be."

Specifically, the "is" that provides the Christian ethical "ought" is the future reality of the new creation. Our calling is to exhibit in our relationships in the here and now God's intentions for human existence, which will be present in their fullness only in the future new community.

While the Christian moral imperative arises out of a future "is," this future does not come as a total contradiction to what is truly natural in the present. As the fullness of God's inten-tion for human relationships, the future community is the completion of what God set forth "in the beginning."

And a crucial aspect of what God has intended for human sexual relationships from the beginning is depicted in the bib-lical creation narratives. This is why reading those stories in the context of the vision of the new creation provides the foundation for our teleological ethical approach to the ques-tion of homosexuality.

## The 'Sin' of Homosexuality

I have asserted that the felt naturalness of a same-sex sexual preference does not in and of itself provide a sufficient rationale for accepting homosexual behavior. But the question remains as to whether or not the preference itself is sinful.

## Sin, Judgment, Acts and Disposition

The search for an answer leads once again to the biblical understanding of sin. Christian theology maintains that the present world is fallen; that is, creation does not yet correspond to the fullness of God's intention. What can be said about humankind as a whole – and even the universe itself (cf. Rom. 8:20-22) – is true of each person as well. Each of us is fallen.

This fallenness extends beyond our specific actions. It encompasses every aspect of our existence, including what might be called our moral disposition (which one day will be conformed to the character of Christ [1 John 3:1-3]) and even the body itself in its mortality (which will be transformed at the resurrection [e.g., Rom. 8:11, 23]). Is this human fallenness "sin"?

In its widest sense, "sin" refers to every aspect of human life that fails to reflect God's design. Viewed from this perspective, fallenness means that we are sinful in the totality of our existence. At the same time, we generally use the word more narrowly. Thus, we speak about "sins;" i.e., specific actions, even transgressions.

The word "sin" immediately conjures up another idea, judgment, that likewise carries two related, yet distinct, meanings. On the one hand, insofar as God one day will transform every dimension of creaturely fallenness, human fallenness comes under divine judgment. On the other hand, the biblical writers consistently reserve the idea of a divine judgment leading to condemnation for sinful acts (e.g., Rom. 2:3; 2 Cor. 5:10; Rev. 20:12).

Putting the two meanings together leads to the conclusion that, as the great physician, God will heal our fallen sinful-

ness in the new creation and, as our judge, God will condemn
our sinful actions. Hence, our fallen disposition is sinful in
that it is foundational to our sinning. But it is our sinful acts –
which bring God's condemnation upon us – that mark us
guilty before God.[26]

## Sexual Desire and Lust

God created us as sexual beings. Within us is the drive to
leave our isolation and enter into relationships with others
and, ultimately, with God. We might term this drive "sexual
desire" because it arises out of our fundamental embodied
existence as sexual creatures.

One aspect of this drive is the "desire for sex;" that is, the
urge to form a genital sexual bond with another person.[27] Certain people find at work in their psyche a desire for sex with
people of the other sex. For other people, the desire for sex
largely, if not exclusively, is targeted toward people of the
same sex. At what point does sin enter into the picture? When
does what belongs to the goodness of our creaturely existence
run counter to God's intention?

It seems that the clearest answer the biblical writers and the
Christian tradition offer is "at the point of lust;" that is, at the
point when a person harbors the desire for sex with someone
who is not his or her spouse (e.g., Matt. 5:27-28). Thus, the
presence in us of both sexual desire and the desire for sex are
the manifestation of the goodness of our creaturely sexuality.
These good gifts, however, can come under the power of sin.

With the incursion of sin, the desire for sex gives birth to
lust. Lust involves allowing the desire for sex to control us so
that the goal of sexual satisfaction has become, in that
moment, our god. Lust also entails the harboring of the desire
to engage in inappropriate sexual expressions, including the
urge to introduce a genital sexual dimension into relationships in which this dimension would be improper.

What we said earlier suggests that all same-sex relationships are an example of one such improper context. To under-

stand this, we must keep in mind that sexual desire in the sense outlined above does not only lie behind the drive to enter into the bond of marriage, it also gives rise to the desire to enter into friendship bonds – even close, intimate friendships. Such friendships may be formed with people of either sex. The desire to bring genital sexual behavior into a same-sex relationship ethically is problematic because it involves treating a friendship like the marital bond.

But what about the situation of those people for whom homoeroticism has become an ongoing, seemingly stable personal disposition?

A proper response requires that we note where the ethical problem actually lies. The presence of sexual desire or the desire for sex within a person's psyche ethically is not problematic. Instead, the moral difficulty emerges when the person involved harbors – and, thus, creates an ongoing urge – to express the desire for sex in acts that are inappropriate, where the "targets" of these desires are potential or actual friends.

Ultimately, it is lust and its outworking in overt acts – not the gender of those toward whom a person might feel drawn (i.e., a person's disposition) – that incur divine condemnation.

## Homosexuality as an Orientation?

One additional question remains to be treated: What about the language of "homosexual orientation" itself? Can we properly talk about "sexual orientation" as separable from sexual acts?

Many evangelical traditionalists find themselves in agreement with proponents of a more open stance at this important point. Both distinguish between a homosexual orientation (or propensity) and homosexual practices.[28] But they do so for quite different reasons.

Gay/lesbian theologians often claim that one's sexual orientation always is good because it is a gift from God. Consequently, the task of the homosexual person is to accept his or her sexual orientation, and this includes acting on the basis of it.

Evangelical traditionalists, in contrast, generally assert that while the Bible condemns homosexual acts, it does not mention the orientation.[29] On this basis, they treat homosexual feelings, attractions, urges, desires and longings as temptations to be mastered, rather than as sins to be confessed. Sin, they add, emerges only when a person acts (whether physically or merely mentally) on these urges. The goal of this approach, of course, is to encourage believers who admit to the ongoing presence of homosexual inclinations, but who are able to resist acting them out.[30]

In a sense, the separation of orientation from behavior is appropriate. It offers a convenient way of differentiating between what truly requires ethical scrutiny (lust and overt acts) and what does not (the desire for sex as a dimension of human existence). To this end, my argument in the previous section drew from a similar distinction, that of disposition versus conduct. Likewise, the pastoral goal of this separation surely is correct. Feeling guilty about what does not incur guilt simply is not justifiable ethically, and it actually can be counterproductive in the journey of discipleship.

While cautiously affirming its utility, we dare not overlook the dangers that lurk in the use of the contemporary language of sexual orientation. I have noted already that social constructivists object to the idea of homosexuality as a transcultural phenomenon. They point out that the idea of a given, stable same-sex sexual orientation that somehow is natural to a certain percentage of people is more the product of a contemporary social construction than an actual essential reality that sociologically or historically can be documented. By using the language of orientation, we risk transposing a construction of contemporary society into indelible scientific fact.

Further, using this language may encourage a significant group of people to construct, perhaps prematurely, their personal identity (the self) on the basis of these socially-based cognitive tools.

One important potential group is today's adolescents. Research in the human sciences suggests that adolescents often move through a stage in their development in which certain same-sex activities are present. The grammar of sexual orientation may lead certain youths to assume on the basis of such experiences that they constitutionally are homosexual. Ruth Tiffany Barnhouse indicates how such an assumption may work to their detriment:

> Adolescence is a period which requires the utmost of young people in working their way through the enormously difficult transition from childhood to adulthood. ... the anxieties surrounding the psychosexual maturation process are severe, and the temptation to opt for less than one is capable of is very great. While it is probably true that one cannot proselytize the invulnerable, there are a great many youngsters whose childhoods have been sufficiently problematic so that homosexuality presented to them as an acceptable alternative would be convincingly attractive.[31]

The "threat," however, is not limited to young people. The widespread use of the language of sexual orientation tempts each of us in a potentially detrimental direction. It may lead us to place our sense of having a sexual orientation, and with it our desire for sex, at the center of our understanding of ourselves and others.

But as certain radical lesbian theologians have asked rhetorically, "Why should the sex of those we desire to sleep with be the determining characteristic of our identity?"[32] Indeed, just as "one's life does not consist in the abundance of possessions" (Luke 12:15), so also there is more to human existence than the desire for sex.

There is yet a deeper theological issue at stake. The uncritical use of the language of sexual orientation may lead us to blindly accept the therapeutic focus rampant in our society. Traditional psychologists routinely assert that homosexual practices, in the end, are the outworking of a psychological maladjustment or a "disorientation."[33] Such assertions, however, replace the moral discussion with a disease model and turn a debate about ethics into a discussion of cures for a psychological illness. David Greenberg offers this sobering reminder:

> Though the Renaissance sodomite was depicted as a monster whose vice signified a repudiation of God and nature, no one suggested that he suffered from a disease and required therapy. ... His repudiation of God and morality was considered volitional; it was his acts, not his physiology or psychology, that made him monstrous.[34]

While Greenberg's choice of the word "monstrous" is unfortunate, his main point is well taken.

The potential problems of "sexual orientation" language ought to give us pause before we too quickly adopt it. Nevertheless, being able to distinguish between homoeroticism and its outworking in thought and overt act – that is, between disposition and conduct – has certain positive benefits in discussing the ethics of homosexuality. Perhaps the best designation, given these considerations, is "sexual preference."

## Homosexual People and Sexual Expression

These conclusions raise one final ethical question: What viable options are there for homoerotic people to express their sexuality? And does the stance argued here mean that a same-sex sexual preference "condemns" a person to a life devoid of sexuality?

### Sexual Chastity

The position taken in these pages leads to only two ethically feasible options for homosexual people: fidelity within (heterosexual) marriage or abstinent singleness. Invariably, proponents of a more open stance toward homosexuality find this proposal uncharitably narrow. They claim such a narrowing of the options for gays and lesbians simply is unfair.

The fairness critique would carry weight if the call for a life characterized by fidelity in marriage or abstinent singleness were directed solely toward homosexual people. The fact, however, is that the elevation of marriage and abstinent singleness merely is the outworking of an ethic of sexual chastity intended for all people without exception.

Some critics do not find this answer at all compelling. They argue that it is far easier for heterosexual than homosexual people to live out such an ethical proposal. James Nelson, for example, claims that this stance "demonstrates lack of sensitivity to the gay person's socially-imposed dilemma." Why? Nelson explains: "The heterosexual's abstinence is either freely chosen for a lifetime or it is temporary until marriage. But the celibacy some Christians would impose on the gay person would be involuntary and unending."[35]

> Christians seek to place life itself – and, hence, sexual expression – under the lordship of Christ. Viewed from this perspective, Christians are convinced that God does care about our sexual conduct.

Other critics add that this proposal erroneously assumes that every homosexual person automatically is called to celibacy. Pamela Dickey Young writes, "In making celibacy mandatory for homosexual persons we violate the traditional Protestant emphasis on celibacy as individual calling."[36]

These objections, however, are wide of the mark. The fact that some people may find it easier to live out an ethical ideal does not mitigate against the ideal itself. Each of us could point to dimensions of the Christian ethic that we find ourselves disadvantaged to follow in comparison with other people. But this does not mean that those who uphold the ideal are treating us unjustly.

Further, proponents of a more open stance toward homosexuality often are overly optimistic about the viability of the
marriage option for heterosexuals. In contrast to such opti-
mism, many single people attest to the fact that, despite their
good intentions and personal willingness, they simply are
unable to find a suitable marriage partner.

Likewise, such objections often confuse celibacy and
abstinence.[37] Young correctly pointed out that only certain
Christians sense a divine call to celibacy, understood as fore-
going marriage and genital sexual intimacy for the purpose of
a special service to God and others.[38] But this is not the same
as my proposal that unmarried homosexual people commit
themselves to abstinence. Unlike celibacy, abstinence in singleness is not a particular calling for certain people, but an
ethical ideal for all who are not married. And unlike celibacy,
which is a chosen, permanent (or semi-permanent) response
to a sensed call from God, the commitment to abstinence in
singleness is a particular, and for many people temporary,
outworking of the overarching call to a life of sexual chastity
that comes to all. This general call to chastity, while remain-
ing the same call, demands a quite different response from
married people than it does from single people.

Finally, the objection that this proposal is unfair rests on a
highly questionable emphasis on rights. John McNeill, for
example, defends homosexual behavior on the basis that
"every human being has a God-given right to sexual love and
intimacy."[39]

This claim, however, displays a faulty understanding of
what a right entails. Love is a relational reality and sexual
love, in particular, requires a partner (a lover). For this reason, no one can claim a personal right to sexual love. Such a
right would demand that a lover exist somewhere for every
person, but no one is entitled to or can be guaranteed a sexual
partner.

Further, such a right would place on someone else the cor-
responding obligation to enter into a sexual relationship with

the person who possesses the right. No one, however, can require that someone else love, let alone become sexually intimate with, him or her.

James Hanigan draws out the implications of these considerations for same-sex relations:

> Since, strictly speaking, there is no positive right to sexual satisfaction, sexual fulfillment and sexual happiness, the human desire for such things and the pursuit of these goods, even the natural human orientation to these goods, cannot itself be a justification for doing just anything to achieve them. ...
>
> Therefore, just because a homosexual relationship may possibly be the only way some people can find, or think they can find, a satisfying degree of humanity in their lives does not make such a relationship morally right by that very fact.[40]

In contrast to contemporary proposals such as McNeill's, the New Testament writers do not build their ethic on an appeal to personal rights. Instead, the early Christian leaders were convinced that discipleship entails a call to follow the example of Jesus, who freely laid aside his personal prerogatives for the sake of a higher good (Phil. 2:5-8; I Peter 2:18-25). This Jesus calls his disciples to give expression to their fundamental human sexuality in ways that bring glory to the God he himself served. As the New Testament writers concluded, his call requires chastity of all people, a chastity that acknowledges the God-given boundaries of genital sexual expression.[41]

But can we truly expect unmarried people to commit themselves to abstinence?

Jesus himself noted that certain people willingly would set aside the sex act for the sake of God's kingdom (Matt. 19:12). The human sciences confirm that sexual activity is not a human necessity, thereby holding open the possibility of abstinence. In the words of Jones and Workman, "There is no basis in behavioral science ... to suggest that abstinence is detrimental to human welfare, or that expression of genital eroticism is necessary for wholeness."[42] Abstinent single Christians stand as living examples of this possibility.

## Homosexual People and Sexual Expression

To commit oneself to abstinence outside of marriage does not mean that single homosexual people are "condemned" to lives devoid of sexual expression. On the contrary, people who are not "sexually active" still experience dimensions of affective sexual expression.

The differentiation between sexual desire and the desire for sex suggests how this is so. As the basis for our innate drive toward bonding, sexuality is operative in the lives of all humans. Hence, our sensed need to bond with other humans, to live in community with others, and even to find God all are aspects of human sexual desire. But as most of our day-to-day relationships indicate, sexual desire does not require that we fulfill the desire for sex; that is, that we engage in sexual intercourse. Rather, as I already have argued, the only context in which the desire for sex properly can be expressed is marriage.

At the same time, we all form non-marital friendship bonds with others. Whenever such bonding occurs, our fundamental sexuality – sexual desire – comes to expression. And as I noted earlier, friendship bonds know no gender boundaries. Hence, our fundamental sexuality readily leads people of the same sex to develop close, even intimate friendships, albeit ones that exclude sexual intimacy in the form of genital relations.

A question commonly asked today is: "Does God really care about whom I sleep with?"

We dare not answer this question in the negative for to do so is to banish God from our sex lives. Rather, Christians seek to understand every aspect of life, including the sexual dimension, within the context of Christian discipleship. Christians seek to place life itself – and, hence, sexual expression – under the lordship of Christ.

Viewed from this perspective, Christians are convinced that God does care about our sexual conduct. And by taking care to live in appropriate sexual chastity, the choice we make as to whom we do – and do not – sleep with becomes a powerful theological statement. This choice speaks loudly about our understanding of ourselves, about our view of the nature of life and, ultimately, about our deepest convictions as to what God is like.

Ultimately, this is the challenge that underlies the discussions about sexual practices so rampant in our society, including the emotionally-charged debate about homosexuality.

*Stanley J. Grenz is Pioneer McDonald Professor of Baptist Heritage, Theology, and Ethics at Carey Theological College and professor of Theology and Ethics at Regent College in Vancouver, B.C.*

## Endnotes

1.  This focus on teleology is also present among proponents of an open stance. See, for example, John J. McNeill, *The Church and the Homosexual*, 3rd ed. (Boston: Beacon Press, 1988), 130-31.

2.  For several contemporary answers to this question, see, for example, the taxonomy and discussion in Peter Coleman, *Gay Christians: A Moral Dilemma* (London: SCM Press, 1989), 191-96, 198-200.

3.  Pim Pronk, *Against Nature? Types of Moral Argumentation Regarding Homosexuality* (Grand Rapids, MI: Eerdmans, 1993), 63-64.

4.  Pronk, *Against Nature?* 65-66.

5.  Maslow notes the implications of this understanding: "It would appear that no single sexual act can per se be called abnormal or perverted. It is only abnormal or perverted individuals who can commit abnormal or perverted acts. That is, the dynamic meaning of the act is far more important than the act itself." Abraham Maslow, "Self-Esteem (Dominance-Feeling) and Sexuality in Women," in *Sexual Behavior and Per-*

*sonality Characteristics*, ed. Manfred F. DeMartino (New York: Citadel Press, 1963), 103.

6. James P. Hanigan, *Homosexuality: The Test Case for Christian Sexual Ethics* (Mahwah, N.J.: Paulist, 1988), 77.

7. For a discussion of such harmful effects, see Jeffrey Satinover, *Homosexuality and the Politics of Truth* (Grand Rapids, Mich.: Baker, 1996), 49-70; Thomas E. Schmidt, *Straight and Narrow? Compassion and Clarity in the Homosexuality Debate* (Downers Grove, IL: InterVarsity, 1995), 100-30.

8. For an example of a slightly more academically credible version of this reasoning, see Michael Keeling, "A Christian Basis for Gay Relationships," in *Towards a Theology of Gay Liberation*, ed. Malcolm Macourt (London: SCM Press, 1977), 104.

9. For a helpful discussion, see Hanigan, 100.

10. Hanigan, 101-2.

11. Hanigan, 102.

12. Max L. Stackhouse, "The Heterosexual Norm," in *Homosexuality and Christian Community*, ed. Choon-Leong Seow (Louisville, KY: Westminster/John Knox, 1996), 141.

13. Hanigan, 99.

14. Stackhouse, "Heterosexual Norm," 141.

15. Ruth Tiffany Barnhouse, *Homosexuality: A Symbolic Confusion* (New York: Seabury, 1977), 172.

16. Hanigan, *Homosexuality*, 100.

17. Edward Batchelor, Jr., *Homosexuality and Ethics* (New York: Pilgrim, 1980), 76.

18. David F. Greenberg, *The Construction of Homosexuality* (Chicago: University of Chicago Press, 1988).

19. See William H. Davenport, "Sex in Cross-Cultural Perspective," in *Human Sexuality in Four Perspectives*, ed. Frank A. Beach (Baltimore: Johns Hopkins University Press, 1977), 156. See also Milton Diamond and Arno Karlen, *Sexual Decisions* (Boston: Little, Brown and Co., 1980), 228.

20. Michel Foucault, *The History of Sexuality: The Use of Pleasure*, vol. 2 (New York: Pantheon Books: 1985), 245.

21. Chris Glaser, *Uncommon Calling: A Gay Christian's Struggle to Serve the Church* (Louisville, KY: Westminster/John Knox, 1996), 181.

22. Christine E. Gudorf, *Body, Sex, and Pleasure: Reconstructing Christian Sexual Ethics* (Cleveland: Pilgrim, 1994), 16.

23. Greenberg, *Construction of Homosexuality*, 492.

24. For a discussion, see Stanley J. Grenz, *The Moral Quest: Foundatiosn of Christian Ethics* (Downers Grove, IL: Inter-Varsity, 1997), 46-47, 76-77.

25. For the author's fuller discussion of this idea, see Grenz, *The Moral Quest*, 223-27.

26. For a more extensive discussion from the author's viewpoint, see Stanley J. Grenz, *Theology for the Community of God* (Nashville: Broadman & Holman, 1995), 257-68.

27. For a similar distinction between sexual desire and the desire for sex, see Hanigan, 143.

28. For an evangelical statement, see for example, Ronald M. Enroth and Gerald E. Jamison, *The Gay Church* (Grand Rapids, MI: Eerdmans, 1974), 137.

29. Hence, Alex Davidson, *The Returns of Love: Letters of a Christian Homosexual* (London: Inter-Varsity, 1970), 38, 41.

30. See, for example, William Consiglio, *Homosexual No More* (Wheaton, IL: Victor, 1991), 36.

31. Barnhouse, *Homosexuality*, 152-53.

32. See, for example, Mary E. Hunt, "Lovingly Lesbian: Toward a Feminist Theology of Friendship," in *Sexuality and the Sacred: Sources for Theological Reflection*, ed. James B. Nelson and Sandra P. Longfellow (Louisville, Ky.: Westminster/John Knox, 1994), 170.

33. For this designation, see Consiglio, *Homosexual No More*, 36.

34. Greenberg, *Construction of Homosexuality*, 335.

35. James B. Nelson, *Embodiment* (Minneapolis: Augsburg, 1978), 208.

36. Pamela Dickey Young, "Homosexuality and Ministry: Some Feminist Reflections," in *Theological Reflections on Ministry and Sexual Orientation*, ed. Pamela Dickey Young (Burling-

ton, Ont.: Trinity Press, 1990), 104.

37. For the author's perspective on this distinction, see Grenz, *Sexual Ethics*,182-85, 196-99.

38. For insight into the positive significance of celibacy, see Jim Cotter, "The Gay Challenge to Traditional Notions of Human Sexuality," in *Towards a Theology of Gay Liberation*, ed. Malcolm Macourt (London: SCM Press, 1977), 67-68.

39. John J. McNeill, "Homosexuality: Challenging the Church to Grow," *Christian Century* 104/8 (11 March 1987): 243. This position was also articulated in McNeill's important work, *The Church and the Homosexual*.

40. Hanigan, 72.

41. A similar understanding of chastity is developed in Donald Goergen, *The Sexual Celibate* (New York: Seabury, 1974), 101-103.

42. Stanton L. Jones and Don E. Workman, "Homosexuality: The Behavioral Sciences and the Church," *Journal of Psychology and Theology* 17/3 (Fall 1989): 224.

CHAPTER 3

# Creation, Covenant, Community ...

## *A Biblical Approach to Sexuality*

### Catherine Clark Kroeger

*B*iblical guidelines for sexual conduct are rooted in our creation in the image of God and our membership in God's covenant community. Our sexuality does not define our basic identity – that is found only in Christ. By his redemptive power, we are made a new creation, above and beyond our sexual nature, and yet rooted to it. God's people are called to sexual purity, regardless of gender, sexual preference or marital status. We also are called to support one another in love.

In 412 BCE, Euripides' play *Andromeda* electrified the Greek-speaking world with a plot so sensational that it has been borrowed countless times since: Boy sees girl about to be slain by monster, falls in love, kills monster, rescues damsel in distress, marries her and lives happily ever after. For days afterward, the streets rang with the chorus that begins, "O love who masters men and gods." This play, so far

63

as is known, first introduced into Greek tradition the literary concept of permanent, romantic love between a man and a woman. Before this, love poems usually had been addressed to people of the same sex.

Euripides' suggestion that a person of the opposite sex appropriately could be one's primary love object did not gain ground all at once. Plato was quite clear in his opinion that truly noble love could exist only between men. Other authors expressed the necessity of male-only love for those of a proper philosophic bent.

The bravest woman was considered more cowardly than the most craven man, and the most virtuous woman baser than the basest man. In short, women were unfit by their very nature for true communion of the soul. One author wrote, "Genuine love has no connection whatsoever with the women's quarters. I deny that it is love that you have felt for women or girls."[1]

Although the love of a mature man for a young boy was the most frequently idealized and extolled, the attachments of grown men to one another drew occasional comment. Famous pairs such as Damon and Pythias and Achilles and Patroclus were glorified because of their devotion to each other. The famed Theban army was said to be composed of homosexual lovers.

While contemporary translations often soft-pedal the sexual innuendoes, the coarse humor of Aristophanes implies that Athenians were known for their participation in same-sex relationships. Attic vase paintings show males copulating with other males who are at various levels of maturity. The liberated Sappho of Lesbos sang of the women she loved. Secluded Athenian women, cruelly denigrated and sexually and socially deprived, often turned to one another, or to artificial means, for gratification.

## Creation

Most Christians would agree that the biblical creation

story is designed to tell us who made the universe, who made human beings, and why. What does it mean to be made in God's image? How can we respect that image in each other and help bring each individual to their fullest potential – spiritually, intellectually and emotionally? What is our relationship and responsibility toward God and other human beings? These are the questions that shape Judeo-Christian thinking.

Genesis 1:26-27 tells us that male and female were created in God's own image, destined to be fruitful and multiply. The thought is repeated in Genesis 5:1-32: "When God created humankind, he made them in the likeness of God. Male and female he created them, and he blessed them and named them 'Humankind' when they were created."

Because they are made in God's image, all people must be respected and their welfare sought. To curse a human being made in the image of God denigrates not only the person, but also God who created all. God showed Peter that he should call no one common or unclean (Acts 10:28).

Traditional Christian theology holds that God exists in three equal persons, of the same substance and yet distinct. There is relationality within the Godhead.

This relationality is part of God's plan for the creation of humanity. God decreed, "It is not good for the man to be alone" (Gen. 2:18). In vain, Adam reviewed all the members of the animal kingdom in search of a suitable companion. Only then was another human formed, drawn from his side, made of the same substance as himself and yet distinct. Finally, there was someone with whom he might share his inmost being. Adam burst into song, "This at last is bone of my bone and flesh of my flesh" (2:23).

This new creature completed the image of God reflected in humanity. How can frail mortals reflect the image of God? Surely not because God has arms and legs; God is spirit, and in the human spirit lies the image of God. God is love, and we are most like God when we love. God is relational, and so we, too, are called to be relational. Both male and female demonstrate aspects of God's being, God's concern for the entire human race, God's own relationality.

The Apostle Paul would refer back to the story of creation in the eleventh chapter of First Corinthians as he addressed a society deeply entrenched with fear and hatred of women. To counter the perception that women were inferior and unfit for the love of noble minds, Paul responded that woman was fashioned of the same stuff as man, sharing the same nature, emotions and aspirations – and integrally bound with him in the body of Christ.

"Nevertheless, in the Lord woman is not independent of man or man independent of woman. For just as woman came from man, so man comes through woman; but all things come from God" (I Cor. 11:11,12).

Women were a "glory," fit partners in the faith and the path of life.

The Bible speaks of a deep unity and interdependence between man and woman. Their union is based on commitment and requires a loosening of other ties. These wonderful spiritual beings who reflect the image of God also are sexual beings. At the end of the creation story, we read the comment, "Therefore a man leaves his father and his mother and clings to his wife, and they become one flesh. And the man and his wife were both naked before one another and were not ashamed" (Gen. 2:23-24). Their nakedness was of both flesh and soul, indicating a willingness to share their inmost being with one another.

The Bible repeatedly represents the union of man and woman as a divinely created gift. A good wife is from the Lord (Prov. 19:14), and a wife of noble character is her husband's crown (Prov. 12:4). The biblical writers fully were aware that marriage not always was good; nevertheless, they make a deliberate effort to promote positive views of marriage and to safeguard its integrity.

Just as human beings most deeply are fulfilled when there is only one divine object for their worship, so too they are

most complete when all of their lifelong devotion is poured
into a single love object. In matters both spiritual and sexual,
the Bible is fiercely exclusivistic:

> Should your springs overflow in the streets, your streams
> of water in the public squares? Let them be yours alone,
> never to be shared with strangers. May your fountain be
> blessed, and may you rejoice in the wife of your youth. A
> loving doe, a graceful deer – may her breasts satisfy you
> always, may you ever be captivated by her love (Prov.
> 5:16-19).

In Malachi, we read that a man's wife ...

> is your companion and your wife by covenant. Did not
> one God make her? Both flesh and spirit are his. And
> what does the one God desire? Godly offspring. So look
> to yourselves, and do not let anyone be faithless to the
> wife of his youth (Mal. 2:14-15).

Husband and wife, therefore, are bound together by a
covenant to which God is a witness (cf. Ezek. 16:8), a
covenant involving community beyond the two marital partners and consent before witnesses.

Woman, therefore, neither was misbegotten male (Aristo-
tle), nor a man who had lived unrighteously in a former existence (Plato), nor formed of an inferior substance and created to play a nasty trick on men, as the Greek poets
declared. Rather, her creation is represented as a blessed provision intended to enrich and complete man. As God is relational, three persons and yet one, so Adam and Eve together
as one flesh reflected the image of God. Only after the creation of the woman did God declare his work to be "very
good" (Gen. 1:31).

## Covenant

The Israelite household was to be built upon the union of
man and woman, bound together by sex and covenant. The
covenant household was to become a haven for the alien and

stranger, a center for instruction and influence to all who entered through its door, a bastion of righteousness, upheld by prayer and commitment to the one true God.

From the resources of this most basic social unit, there was to be outreach to the needy or distressed. The influence of the household on the political, economic and social betterment of the community is well described in Proverbs 31, which outlines the activities of the valiant woman whose husband and household safely trust in her. The venture is a cooperative one, involving both wife and husband.

Old Testament covenants intimately are connected with issues of sexuality. The covenants promised health, offspring and blessing as the fruit of conformity to God's laws. Sexuality, revealed in Scripture as an enormously powerful force, can bring great harm when misused. Particularly in Leviticus 18, we find a review of destructive expressions of sexuality: those types of behavior considered defiling not only to the individual, but also to the community at large.

> Precisely because of the covenant relationship, God's people were not to engage in certain sexual practices. If they were to be included in the community, they were obligated to maintain covenantal standards of behavior.

Donald Wold recently has pointed out that Leviticus 18 contains a form of covenant similar to the suzerainty treaties of the Hittites.[2] The same form of contract also is discernible in the covenants of Exodus 20 and Joshua 24. The Levitical passage both begins and ends with the identification of the suzerain, "I am the Lord your God" (v. 4, 30), a formula that recurs twice more within the 29 verses (v. 6, 21). In verse 3 is a historical prologue reminding the vassal people of God's saving acts and the provision of a new land. Then comes the obligation that Israel was to be dissociated from the lifestyle of its neighbors in Egypt and Canaan, an instruction reiterated six times in chapter 18 (twice in vs. 3, also in vs. 24, 26-27, 30).

> You must not live according to the customs of the nations
> I am going to drive out before you ... I am the Lord your
> God who has set you apart from the nations. You are to
> be holy to me because I, the Lord, am holy and I have set
> you apart from the nations to be my own (Lev. 20:22-26).

To this is added the positive command, "You must perform my statutes and observe my ordinances" (v. 4). The covenant people, called to serve the one true God, were to retain their distinctiveness in the midst of a society permeated with very different values and practices. Here is a call to conform to God's image in holiness. Ultimately, the mandate called for likeness to God: "You shall be holy for I the Lord your God am holy" (Lev. 19:2).

Verses 6 to 23 of Leviticus 18 detail specific stipulations regarding sexual and reproductive behavior. These include the forbiddance of incest (vv. 6-16), bigamy (v. 18), intercourse with a menstruant (v. 19), adultery (v. 20), offering seed to Moloch (v. 21), and bestiality (v. 23). Verses 24 to 28 spell out the rationale for the prohibitions: Such behavior pollutes the land and endangers the community. The treaty concludes with the penalty for offenders – to be cut off from the covenant people.

Within the extended passage is embedded, "Do not lie with a male as one lies with a woman; it is an abhorrence" (Lev. 18:22). The Hebrew word *to' evah*, here translated "abhorrence," occurs in the book of Leviticus exclusively with reference to sexual activity. Regarding the classification of intercourse with a menstruant as an abomination, it must be remembered that in a primitive society, where one type of gynecological condition quite easily might be confused with another, the instruction had far greater validity than would be the case in our contemporary world. D. F. Greenberg wrote

> [t]hat intercourse with a menstruating woman is also clas-
> sified as an abomination along with homosexuality is an

indication not ... that the latter offense was considered
trivial, but rather that the former was considered
extremely grave. However silly they may seem to contemporary rationalists, menstrual taboos are taken very
seriously in many primitive societies. Late biblical Palestine was one of them. We would do well to remember that
this instruction is not repeated in the New Testament,
though the strictures against incest and homosexuality are
clearly maintained.[3]

When the term *to' evah* is used in the plural, it refers to
several types of sexual behavior, but in the singular it is used
in Leviticus only for same-gender intercourse. This is true
both of the 18th and 20th chapters, where there is a similar
review of prohibitions regarding sexual and reproductive mis-
conduct. Like the covenant of chapter 18, chapter 20 also is
introduced with the words, "I am the Lord your God," a formula frequently recurring throughout the passage and precisely the terms in which the covenant was introduced at the
giving of the Ten Commandments (Ex. 20:2). Here it is written, "If a man lies with a man as one lies with a woman, both
of them have done what is abhorrent (*to' evah*)" (Lev. 20:13).

Precisely because of the covenant relationship, God's people were not to engage in certain sexual practices. If they
were to be included in the community, they were obligated to
maintain covenantal standards of behavior. Prophets and
priests demanded that the faith community hold one another
accountable for the preservation of the laws of Israel. It is in
this context of maintaining likeness to God and fidelity to the
covenant community that same-sex union is prohibited in
Leviticus 18 and 20.

In the Hebrew Scriptures, homosexuality is not singled out
as particularly reprehensible – it is mentioned seldom and
usually in connection with other inappropriate activities. The
New Testament, as well, includes homosexual conduct as part
of much larger discussions concerning a wide range of sexual
conduct.

Fornication and adultery are the two behaviors most consistently condemned in both Testaments. This is congruent with some of the contemporary sociological studies that indicate not only that the prevalence of exclusively homosexual people is quite low, but that the promiscuity rate is at least as high among heterosexuals. Any discussion of biblical directives on homosexuality also must include an acknowledgement of the far larger problem of other kinds of sexual impropriety.

It is remarkable that the section of Leviticus regarding social and sexual behavior begins and ends with a reminder of God's covenant with Israel. Just as in the Sinai covenant, God's role as deliverer and suzerain is outlined and then followed by the commitment required from God's people. Sexual behavior is a major element of the covenantal

> God's people must call each other to accountability. Those who engage in inappropriate sexual relationships wrong not only themselves, but also the corporate body of Christ.

union and can be found within virtually all of the biblical covenants.

## Community

It sometimes is argued that the New Testament does not specifically address the issue of same-sex commitments between mature, faithful adults because such relationships were unknown. This is to ignore a substantial number of literary attestations for both male and female unions.

As already mentioned, the famed Theban army was said to have consisted of devoted male pairs. In every major city in Palestine, archaeologists have unearthed clay vessels from the Roman period depicting homoerotic acts. During the lifetime of Paul, same-sex marriages were in vogue at Rome, especially among young males of patrician families. The Emperor Nero himself participated in two homosexual wedding ceremonies, once as the bride and once as the groom. The Egyptian princess Berenice married a woman named Mesopotamia.

Every sort of sexual experiment was tried until the Imperial City itself reeled with revulsion. Interestingly enough, aversion to sexual activity started among the pagans, not the Christians. In the ensuing centuries, the population of Rome dropped from a million to six hundred thousand, partly because people had lost interest in sex.

Centuries before the New Testament era, Plato had glorified permanent same-sex attachments. He insisted that truly noble love only could exist between two males, and he projected the ideal as lasting throughout the entire lifetime of each. Some of these same-sex unions were formalized with wedding ceremonies. The binding words used in these rituals have been preserved in ancient texts.

The New Testament writers hardly could have been ignorant of these social patterns. Paul, Apostle to the Gentiles, wrote at the height of Rome's paganism and promiscuity. If newly-converted Gentiles came to Christianity with ambivalence on the matter of sexuality, it scarcely is to be wondered.

In the opening of his epistle to the Romans, Paul describes those who exchanged the glory of God for other images, worshipping and serving the creature rather than the Creator. Women and men turned to other paths of sexual expression than those given by God. They rejected God and followed "the lusts of their hearts to impurity, to the degrading of their bodies among themselves. ... For this reason God gave them up to degrading passions. Their women exchanged natural intercourse for unnatural, and in the same way also the men, giving up natural intercourse with women, were consumed with passion for one another. Men committed shameless acts with men and received in their own persons the due penalty for their error" (Rom. 1:24, 26-27). [Some have argued that the phrase *para fusin,* here translated "unnatural" or "against nature," does not refer to people drawn toward members of the same sex. However, *para fusin* commonly is used in Greek literature to designate homosexual behavior.]

Paul treats sexual conduct most extensively in 1 Corinthians 5-7. The passage begins with his recommendation for handling a case of flagrant *porneia* – about which the congregation has been rather smug in its own broadmindedness. After a stinging rebuke, he calls on the entire faith community to treat the individual redemptively, but categorically to repudiate the behavior. The term *porneia*, usually translated *fornication*, can imply any inappropriate, lewd, immoral or indecent sexual conduct, including homosexual actions.

Paul condemns many other behaviors – deceit, craftiness, gossip, slander, insolence and rebellion, to name just a few. Paul noted that those who engaged in such deeds "even applauded others who practice them" (Rom. 1:32). Fortunately, Paul does not stop with excluding individuals whose behavior is unacceptable. After naming those who fall short of God's standards, he writes, "And such were some of you, but you are washed, you are sanctified, you are justified in the name of the Lord Jesus Christ and in the Spirit of our God" (I Cor. 6:10). God is in the business of making people new, and we together are heirs of the promise. A man dying of AIDS once asked, "Are homosexuals to be excluded from the community of faith?" Richard B. Hays answered, "Certainly not. But anyone who joins such a community should know that it is a place of transformation, of discipline, of learning, and not merely a place to be comforted or indulged."[4] Yes, we are frail forgiven sinners seeking to live out God's will in our lives.

We cannot divorce our sexual conduct from the family of faith. In keeping with the covenantal concerns of the Pentateuch, Paul speaks of certain types of sexual conduct, including same-sex intercourse, as a spiritual hazard to the faith community (6:9). The heirs of God's kingdom are redirected to chastity, sanctification, reconciliation and justification. The First Epistle to Timothy likewise lists homosexual union as disqualifying conduct in the household of God.

Paul, while granting the right to remain unmarried, insists that woman is the appropriate soulmate of man. "Neither is the man without the woman, nor the woman without the man in the Lord" (I Cor. 11:11). As Christians, our essential being is not defined by our actions or sexual preferences, but by our redemption in Christ.

God's people must call each other to accountability. Those who engage in inappropriate sexual relationships wrong not only themselves, but also the corporate body of Christ. Paul pointed out that a little leaven exerts its influence on the entire mass of dough (5:6). Lisa Sowle Cahill wrote:

"Early Christians differed from the Greco-Roman philosophers in that the focus of concern over promiscuity was the unity of the community, not the perfection of the individual. Members of the community were addressed not as individual citizens with control over their own bodies and households, but as members of the body of Christ, the community in whom Christ's Spirit dwells."[5]

Our sexual conduct intimately is related to others in the faith community. It matters, then, what we tell others about the legitimacy of relationships not sanctified by Scripture, how we accord acceptance for behavior that may have repercussions not now fully understood.

The First Epistle to the Corinthians is deeply concerned with unity at many different levels – whether healing squabbles occasioned by loyalty to different leaders or addressing those who created a dichotomy between body and soul. Like the Levitical passages, the author addresses activities that violate covenant community. The disruptive behaviors include sexual impurity, idolatry, adultery, same-sex intercourse, robbery, greed, drunkenness, verbal abuse and rape (6:9-10).

Our concern as Christians should be both for people outside the church and inside it. Inappropriate sex can do great harm to others and to ourselves. Our present knowledge cannot entirely explain the psychological, social, emotional and spiritual influence that sexual union has upon us for good or ill.

How can it both nourish our souls and yet destroy us? This is indeed a mystery (Eph. 5:32), one we can commit to an all-wise and loving God. If, however, sexual actions affect our deepest nature, then we must tread very carefully upon paths we do not fully comprehend. Our bodies, Paul says, are the temples of the Holy Spirit. He adds, "You are not your own, you are bought with a price. Therefore glorify the Lord in your bodies, which are the Lord's" (I Cor. 6:19-20).

When Paul rhetorically asks, "Shall I take the members of the body of Christ and make them members of a prostitute?" (I Cor. 6:15), his reply (v. 16) uses the word *kollao*, literally, "Absolutely not! He that is glued to a prostitute is one body. Do you not know that the Scripture says 'the two shall be one flesh'?" *Kollao* means to glue or cement something, but also to bind one person or thing to another, to join fast, to unite, to bind indissolubly. The apparently casual union has claimed more from each participant than they might have imagined. Even coition with a prostitute makes her one flesh with the body of Christ, glued both to the individual and to the entire community. Far from purely recreational sex, it brings about a spiritual tie between the harlot and the body of believers who compose the church – a sobering thought to those who maintain that what they do in the bedroom is no one else's business.

Paul goes on to point out that the one who is glued to the Lord is one spirit with the Lord (I Cor. 6:17). The text continues, "Flee immorality. Every sin which an individual does is outside the body, but the one who is engaged in immorality sins against the body itself" (I Cor. 16:18). The implication is that, through sin, one inflicts upon oneself a spiritual, psychological or even physical injury.

One may ask if the reference to immorality (*porneia*) as a sin against the body refers only to an individual body or to the corporate body of Christ. Perhaps the answer is found in

the previous comment that a little leaven exerts its influence
on the entire mass of dough (I Cor. 5:6). Certainly here, Paul
has in mind the total personality as body and he indicates that
our sexuality lies far closer to who we really are than we
might imagine.

He further maintains that sex has the power to sanctify the
unbelieving partner in a marriage, a further indication that
sexual union is not merely physical and contractual, but also
profoundly spiritual (I Cor. 7:14). Sexual behavior affects our
inmost being in ways that other behaviors do not. Derrick
Sherwin Bailey writes,

> [t]he Apostle denies that coitus is, as the Corinthians
> would have it, merely a detached and (as it were) periph-
> eral venereal function involving no more than an appro-
> priate exercise of the genital organs. On the contrary, he
> insists that it is an act which, by reason of its very nature,
> engages and expresses the whole personality in such a
> way as to constitute a unique mode of self-disclosure and
> self-commitment.[6]

There is no record of Jesus having ever explicitly
addressed the issue of homosexuality, and there is no discussion of sexual orientation as such in the New Testament.
Jesus, however, consistently propounded a view of marriage
as lifelong, total commitment to one's spouse. The disciples
reacted with dismay and declared, "If such is the relationship
of a man with the wife, it is not beneficial to be married"
(Matt. 19:10). Jesus readily conceded that this calling was not
for everyone and could not be accepted by all. The challenge,
however, remains as a goal and ideal for his followers.

Jesus had a remarkable felicity in accepting people while
rejecting certain behaviors. He received tax gatherers and
challenged them to restore the wealth they wrongfully had
wrested from others. The Pharisees condemned him for
allowing a fallen woman to touch him, while Jesus accepted
both her and her tears of repentance. In the story of the
woman taken in adultery, the human being was affirmed,

while the behavior was repudiated. The Bible condemns sinful practices, not people. While we may not be able to control our inclinations, we are expected to control our actions.

Desires, lusts and passions frequently are addressed in the New Testament. In Christ, there are new relationships and new ways of dealing with desire. The writer of Colossians is aware that mere prohibition is of no value in controlling physical passions (Col. 2:12). There is a need to rechannel sexual energies. Believers are called upon to put off as dead *porneia*, impurity, illicit passion, evil lusts and greed (3:5). These are to be transformed into new spiritual qualities, including compassion, kindness, humility, gentleness, patience and love (3:12-14).

> Each of us is called to a life of sexual renunciation and purity. Together, we struggle with lusts, urges and desires. Yet, we are all, including our homosexual brothers and sisters, called to move beyond the limitations of the flesh to the liberty of God.

But what about those who feel no attraction to a person of the opposite sex? Can they not find fulfillment? If we are to say that God's plan is for lasting heterosexual union between male and female, if we are to say that overt genital expression of same-sex love is forbidden by Scripture, are we not being unfair?

The people of Ezekiel's day asked the same sort of question: "Yet you say, 'The way of the Lord is unfair.' Hear now, O house of Israel: Is my way unfair? Is it not your ways that are unfair" (Ezek. 18:25, 29)? Are we truly wise enough to understand the ways of God and the ways of the human heart?

Both the Hebrew Bible and the New Testament celebrate the loyalty and devotion of same-sex friendship, but stop short of endorsing genital expression. Even that most articulate tribute to homophilia in the ancient world, Plato's Symposium, ultimately concludes that same-sex love reaches its highest form in perfect celibacy.

But should we call people to renounce an essential part of their nature?

Jesus himself renounced many legitimate needs in view of the higher priority of the claims of the kingdom. He denied himself food, sleep and a permanent place of lodging, even as he called his followers to show active concern for the hungry, the poor and the homeless. He challenged his disciples to a similar renunciation of their personal needs and desires in all-consuming commitment to the Good News of God's redemptive love.

"If any one would come after me, let that one deny her or himself and take up her/his cross and follow me. Whoever wishes to save their life shall lose it, and whoever loses their life for my sake shall find it" (Matt. 16:24).

Not only did Jesus commend to his adherents fasting instead of food, watching instead of sleep, proclamation of the Kingdom rather than a fixed place of residence; but he pointed out that some had made themselves eunuchs for the sake of the kingdom of heaven (Matt. 19:12). In other words, they sacrificed active sexual expression for other values. Jesus maintained that the gospel must be placed ahead of even legitimate family relationships. As the writer of Ecclesiastes had observed, "There is a time to embrace, and a time to refrain" (3:5).

Each of us is called to a life of sexual renunciation and purity. Together, we struggle with lusts, urges and desires. Yet we are all, including our homosexual brothers and sisters, called to move beyond the limitations of the flesh to the liberty of God. Admittedly theirs is the far greater sacrifice, and that is why those who make such a choice deserve the respect and support of fellow Christians. Theirs is a special place in God's provision. The prophet Isaiah proclaimed that the covenant extended to all who would obey, and then displayed a special sensitivity for those suffering sexual deprivation.

Let no eunuch complain, "I am only a dry tree." For thus says the Lord: To the eunuchs who keep my sabbaths, who choose the things that please me and hold fast my covenant, I will give, in my house and within my walls, a monument and a name better than sons and daughters; I will give them an everlasting name that shall not be cut off (Isa. 56:4-5).

Holiness constitutes a condition of set-apartness, separation from the ways of the world and consecration to God (2 Cor. 6:16-18). "This is the will of God, even your sanctification," Paul wrote to the Thessalonians, "that you abstain from porneia, that each one of you know how to control your own body in holiness and honor, not with lustful passion like the Gentiles who do not know God; that no one wrong or exploit a brother or sister in this matter [i.e. sexual conduct], because the Lord is an avenger in all things, just as we have already told you beforehand and solemnly warned you. For God did not call us to impurity but in holiness. Therefore whoever rejects this rejects not human authority but God, who also gives his Holy Spirit to you" (I Thess. 4:3-7).

Scripture makes a strong differentiation between sex that enriches the human spirit and that which degrades it. The Bible speaks candidly of the sordid uses to which sex can be put: manipulation, exploitation, violence and aggression. It can debase a relationship, demean a person and violate a soul.

What should be our stance toward those practicing unscriptural conduct? Faithful leaders in the Judeo-Christian tradition are expected to proclaim God's law and defend it. The covenant of priesthood was extended to Phinehas precisely because of his insistence on protecting the sexual morality and safety of Israel. John the Baptist, last and greatest of the prophets, lost his life because of his defense of the sexual standards of the covenant community. Today's leaders, too, bear a responsibility for the flock.

## Conclusion

As we discuss altering church doctrine to include same-sex union, we would be wise to remember that Scripture provides guidelines for sexual conduct in the very same context as it describes our creation in the image of God and membership in God's covenant community.

If the Bible is the inspired Word of God, our only infallible rule of faith and practice, then are we wise enough to set up guidelines or ethical principles of sexual conduct outside those outlined in Scripture? Are we wise to look to modern scientific research when its findings are so contradictory?

Today one can find support both for the claim that homosexual orientation is genetic and that it is produced by environmental factors. There is wide divergence of opinion as to the prevalence of homosexuality in the general population. Regardless, the prevalence, or lack thereof, of certain practices in society does not commend them to the covenant community for emulation. We are called to be a counterculture. Sexual conduct is woven into the warp and woof of the covenants, and sexual purity is a distinguishing characteristic of God's people.

We know the directives given in Scripture; we can only guess at the reasons lying behind those mandates. As the heavens are high above the earth, so are God's ways and understanding higher than ours. God has dealt faithfully with believers for thousands of years; and the Scriptures have been our guide through vast territories we did not understand.

That same faithful God still reveals guidelines to provide for our safety and ultimate joy. We are given "what," but only a very limited comprehension of "why." Yet, we ignore God's precepts at our peril. If there are dangers inherent in certain behaviors, whether physical, mental or spiritual, then we need to point God's people to another path. Permissiveness at the wrong point is betrayal.

The Bible instructs us to lead celibate lives outside of faithful heterosexual marriage. Yet, there are other clear directives that all believers should heed. We are a fellowship of people committed to Jesus Christ and, as such, we belong to one another. Within the church, the gay believer is one with the grandmother of 12; the grieving widow is one with the believing Lesbian. We are together the body of Christ and must pray for and support one another. To live a life of celibacy takes special grace, Paul tells us, and part of this grace is the caring concern of other Christians. If a person struggles with issues of sexuality, there must be a caring community where that individual safely can share their pain and find loving compassion. The Bible condemns gossips, troublemakers and unloving, judgmental critics far more consistently than it does homosexuals.

The Bible also is very clear that we bear responsibility toward those who are ill. "I was sick and you did not take care of me," Jesus says; "Truly I tell you, just as you did not do it to one of the least of these, you did not do it to me" (Matt. 26:42, 45). Despite the biblical command to lay hands upon the sick, many people recoil from AIDS victims in horror. Where the Good Samaritan poured on oil and wine, we pour on reproach and scorn.

Although there may be deep love and commitment in a same-sex union, such a union does not include both male and female, of bonding to one who is wholly other. We must be careful not to encourage those made in God's image to settle for less. Our sexuality does not define our basic identity – that is found only in Christ. By his redemptive power, we are made a new creation, above and beyond our sexual nature and yet rooted to it. Regardless of gender, sexual preference or marital status, all of us are challenged to a life that puts the kingdom of heaven before our own physical needs and desires. Clearly, not all have the same calling, and this is stressed both by Jesus and the Apostle Paul. Some are given the gift of marriage and some of celibacy. There is a calling for each of us.

Is your congregation one in which folk will stand beside those in need, to love them, to include them, to weep with them and to affirm them? Can you reach out arms of love to hug them, to hold their hand, to let them feel the bond of oneness in Christ? Can you extend the grace of touch and embrace to those who need it most? Would a person dealing with issues of homosexuality dare trust you?

Only so can we be God's covenant people.

*Catherine Clark Kroeger is president and co-founder of the Cape Cod Institute for Christian Studies, and adjunct associate professor at Gordon Conwell Theological Seminary.*

## Endnotes

1.  Plutarch Amores 750C, Loeb Classical Library translation; See also Lucian Erotes 51, 39-40, Anthologia Palatina XII, 245.

2.  Donald F. Wold, *Out of Order: Homosexuality in the Blible and Ancient Near East.* Grand Rapids: Baker Books, 1988.

3.  David F. Greenberg, *The Construction of Homosexuality.* Chicago: University of Chicago Press, 1988. p. 196.

4.  Richard B. Hays, "Awaiting the Redemption of our Bodies," *Sojourners* (July 20, 1991),pp. 20-21.

5.  Lisa Sowle Cahill, "Sexual Ethics: A Feminist Biblical Perspective," *Interpretation.* Vol. XLIX, No. 1 (Jan, 1995) pp. 11, 12.

6.  Derrick Sherwin Bailey, *Sexual Relations in Christian Thought.* New York: Harper and Row, 1959, p. 9-10.

CHAPTER 4

# The Social Construction
of Homosexuality

**Alan Storkey**

*T* *he term "homosexual" is misleading, first
because identity does not rest in one's sexuality,
but in our full human relationship with God and
others, and second because very few people are
exclusively "homosexual." The cultural idiom that
males either are "men" or else they are gay, together
with the tendency to identify people as either "homosexual" or "straight," has created and encouraged
much homophobia. Both dichotomies are wrong.*

## The Search for the 'Homosexual'

The search for "the homosexual" emerged only in the 19th
century. Before then, in many different cultures, homosexual
behavior was common in some cases and rare in many others,
but it usually was not understood as something unique to a
class of people who were different in nature.

In some cultures, homosexual activity was built into the
process of growing up. In New Guinea, where boys largely
are brought up by women, male maturity is "passed on"
through a homosexual relationship, usually with an uncle. In

Dahomey, male and female homosexuality both are common and considered normal in adolescence when the sexes are segregated; at later stages, they are much less common and, because they are considered undesirable, concealed.[1]

In these and other cases where there are early homosexual experiences, heterosexuality and marriage are considered natural and normal later in life, and no special class of people is identified and created. Why, then, was a special class of people identified in the late 19th century?

In the 1800s, attempts were made to discover the "nature" of things, including the state, the economy or Man. The workings of an entity were analyzed in an almost mechanical way. In mid-century, for example, Phrenology involved the belief that, by reading bumps on the head, a person's character could be determined.

This way of thinking also began to occur in relation to sexuality. Johann Ludwig Gasper, Karl Heinrich Ulrich and Karoly Maria Benkert argued that homosexuality could be innate. Benkert first used the term "homosexual."

The focus on homosexual "nature" was reinforced from two sides. On the one hand, those who feared homosexual behavior found the process of naming and vilifying a group the best way of keeping them at a distance. At a popular level, this occurred by calling them monsters, beasts or poofs, but it occurred at a more academic level by searching for the distinguishing characteristic that marked the "nature" or, sometimes, the "unnature" of the homosexual.

On the other hand, those with homosexual experience sought to validate their behavior by looking for a natural explanation. Reading Havelock Ellis's *Sexual Inversion* "brought home" to F.O. Mathiessen that he was inverted "by nature," not because he had been seduced by other boys at school.[2] The conclusion probably was incorrect, but it is easy to see how it would provide some psychological stability. Alfred Binet and others who claimed homosexuality was acquired rather than innate eventually were ignored.

Initially, physiology was explored as the causal basis for homosexuality. Explanations focused on body type or physique and some studies occurred that identified factors, including lower average body weight and more feminine physical characteristics. The physiological argument hopelessly was flawed, however, for this stereotyping of homosexuals obviously broke down. Empirical findings show that gays are of every size and physical type.

## Naturalism as a Cultural Idiom

The drive behind the physiological and psychological search was to uncover the nature of homosexuality. "It" and "they" were seen as unnatural and, therefore, in need of an explanation.

In straightforward terms, homosexuality is "unnatural" because the male sexual organ is designed to fit the female sexual organ, and sperm combine with eggs to produce offspring. This seems basic to creation and difficult to reject as a basic part of the human condition. Recent attempts to do so, like growing a fetus outside the womb or hormonal manipulation, are manipulating a sophisticated natural (or, better, "created") process in rather crude ways.

> The label of "homosexual" does great damage, both in the attitudes of heterosexual members of the population who are prepared to label and even hate this group, but also among those who call themselves homosexual. There is nothing warranting the identification of homosexual as a natural condition. The noun must go.

This purposed structure of genital sex, therefore, seems clearly heterosexual and few would deny this. This is the simple and irrefutable Christian argument: God created them male and female and they are different. "Natural" sex, in straightforward terms, is that between a man and a woman.

But the culture of Naturalism sets off in a different direction, even when it makes the same point. Nature often is seen as a basic, even sacred, category of understanding. What is natural is good and what is unnatural is bad. When this emphasis is tagged on to the simple point above, the conclusion is that heterosexual sex is good and homosexual sex is bad. Sex is seen as a drive that naturally is directed by men at women. Naturalism traditionally has been a patriarchal view – men as subjects, women as objects. In this view, men are heterosexual and sex is an expression of one's nature and, therefore, is good, whatever kind of relations with women are involved. Prostitution and male promiscuity merely are an expression of masculine nature. This has been the culturally-dominant view among males for centuries.

The Naturalistic understanding of sex has created a permissive moral code down the ages that has allowed men especially to justify whatever heterosexual activities they undertake. Cruelty, abuse and rape, not to mention selfishness and insensitivity, often have marked male heterosexual attitudes. The process, therefore, often has validated male attitudes toward women, however wrong and evil, while scapegoating homosexual activity as "unnatural." Rather than love and faithfulness, the emphasis is on being heterosexual and "normal," versus homosexual and perverted.

This, of course, is very different from the Christian understanding that sex within marriage as an expression of love is good, but that adultery and fornication are bad. Christianity has a much more modulated view of heterosexual sex that also views lust as sinful.

There is another problem. Naturalism focuses on our nature, especially as male and female. An important response to this emphasis has been to define masculinity in ways that offer security and identity. Cultural definitions of masculinity have been examined in many studies, but one of the most powerful components is to define it in terms of sex with women. In many cultures sex with a woman is regarded as an initiation into manhood.

In this view, for a man to have sex with another man, or not at all, is akin to not being a man. The position is illogical since homosexuality is defined as sexual activity between men, but the fear has been an important part of male cultural identity for a long time. Indeed, it offers us a theory of homophobia. For if identity as a man depends on having sex with a woman, then sexual arousal toward another man must induce tremendous levels of fear. Those who have experienced same-sex arousal, but are predominantly heterosexual, may see this as a potential curse and will view open homosexuals as less than men.

Another weakness of Naturalism is its in-built quest for the expression of sexual nature. De Sade stated the view well 200 years ago:

> It makes absolutely no difference whether one enjoys a girl or a boy. ... no inclinations or tastes can exist in us save the ones we have from Nature ... she is too wise and too consistent to have given us any which could ever offend her. The penchant for sodomy is the result of physical formation, to which we contribute nothing, and which we cannot alter.[3]

Here we see that Naturalism ultimately is permissive. If our nature dictates, then how can we do other?

Finally, we note the power of Naturalism in creating a label and an identity. Attempting to find what makes a person homosexual by nature teaches people to think of *being* homosexual. Homosexuality becomes an identity, one that makes people different. It also, to a considerable extent, has become the internalized identity of those who apply the label to themselves. If they "are homosexual," then there is an extensive process of developing a new identity, which often is traumatic and difficult. If I am a homosexual, the argument goes, then how can I do other than live as homosexuals do?

But is it possible that this assumed "identity" is not the

case? There is, in fact, a great deal of evidence that young Mr. Mathiessen was mistaken: He actually had been seduced by older boys at school and then had come to accept homosexuality as his nature.

The label of "homosexual" does great damage, both in the attitudes of heterosexual members of the population who are prepared to label and even hate this group, but also among those who call themselves homosexual. There is nothing warranting the identification of homosexual as a natural condition. The noun must go.

## The National Sexual Survey and its Conclusions

The study *Sexual Behaviour in Britain*[4] gives the most comprehensive picture yet of national homosexual behavior and it is worth reviewing its conclusions, which confirm the argument above in several important ways. It was a weighted, random, confidential sample of about 20,000 and is likely to give results reflecting actual attitudes and patterns with limited error.

First, we consider the scale of homosexual attitudes and experience. There has been a tendency for the gay community to talk up the figures for homosexuality because it suggests that it is more "normal" or "natural" than many are prepared to accept. There is a need for safety in numbers.

The Kinsey studies, which for a long time have dominated this area, suggested that approximately 4 percent of the male population were exclusively homosexual, while another 9 percent had been predominantly homosexual for at least one period in their lives. This produced the conclusion that 13 percent of the sample were, at least for a time, predominantly homosexual, and many of the rest had had some homosexual experience and arousal. The sample, however, consisted of volunteers who tended to be Californian and predominantly students, factors that might bias the sample.

Without entering into that debate directly, we note that the British study employed random sampling techniques that

| Sexual Behaviour in Britain: Study Results | | |
|---|---|---|
| Individual has had... | M | F |
| any homosexual experience | 6.1% | 3.4% |
| a homosexual partner | 3.5% | 1.7% |
| a homosexual partner in the last 5 years | 1.4% | 0.6% |
| a homosexual partner in the last 1-2 yrs | 1.1% | 0.4% |
| only same sex attraction | 0.5% | 0.3% |
| only same sex experience | 0.4% | 0.1% |

gave a much better chance of accuracy.

The survey used two techniques for getting information – interview and a self-completion booklet. The latter had slightly higher figures, roughly consistent with the interview ones, and we will use them (see table above). 6.1 percent of men, or 1 in 17, had some homosexual experience, which was "any kind of contact with another person which you felt was sexual (it could be just kissing or touching, or intercourse, or any other kind or form of sex)," the widest possible definition.[5]

Only 3.5 percent, or 1 in 29 men, had ever had a homosexual partner (defined as same-sex genital contact), and 1.4 percent, or 1 in 72 men, had had a homosexual partner in the last five years.[6] 3.4 percent of women, or 1 in 29, have had any lesbian experience. 1.7 percent, or 1 in 59, ever have had a lesbian partner and 0.6 percent, or 1 in 167, women have had a lesbian partner in the last five years.

These are rather sober figures, involving a far smaller proportion of the population than Kinsey suggested. Only one in a hundred people will have had a homosexual partner in the last five years. But this point about the scale of homosexual behavior is less important for our study than the findings about whether homosexual relations are exclusive. For if there is a type who naturally is homosexual, then it hardly would be evidenced in bisexual attraction. 93.3 percent of men and 93.6 percent of women had only heterosexual attraction, leaving 6 percent to 7 percent with homosexual attraction at some time, however slight.

Here we note that nine out of 10 of these men and 19 out of 20 of these women also had heterosexual attraction or experience. In other words, the exclusive homosexual is quite rare.[7]

If we look at those who only had same-sex attraction, the figure falls to 0.5 percent of men (1 in 200) and 0.3 percent of women (1 in 330). The figures for only same-sex experience were 0.4 percent and 0.1 percent, where experience is "any kind of contact with another person that you felt was sexual."[8] These figures undercut the idea of homosexuality as a natural condition of some consequence and reveal how weak the idea of a "natural homosexual" really is.

There are a number of conclusions we can draw. First, homosexuality is experienced by a small minority. Second, the historical concern with identifying "the homosexual" is misplaced since the overwhelming majority of those with same-sex experience also have other-sex experience. What we are better considering is a range of experience occurring in mixed-gender contexts, predominately heterosexual but including some homosexual contacts, often quite limited. "Half the men and two-thirds of the women who report having a same-sex partner during their lifetime have had only one."[9] Third, the data suggests that middle-aged men have tended to have more homosexual experience and that it usually occurred at a relatively young age.[10]

There is another important finding that relates to promiscuity, often associated with homosexuality. Overall, levels of promiscuity among heterosexual men roughly are comparable to that among homosexual men.[11] Given the overwhelming size of the heterosexually experienced group, this leads to the conclusion that promiscuity primarily is a heterosexual problem.

## Post-Modern Theory

The old Naturalistic understandings now have been subject to extensive criticisms in the sociological literature.[12] Gradually, studies of homosexuality showed the social dynamics through which particular outcomes were possible.[13] Now, a whole stream of writers sees, in Caplan's terms, the "cultural construction of sexuality" as the normal pattern of gay and lesbian relationships. These relationships are understood more as matters of choice than as necessary inner drives.

The literature gradually has opened up into an exploration of a whole range of gay and lesbian lifestyles that no longer are seen as "natural," but which are part of a modern relativist culture. No longer, for example, is there a search for an innate psychology because it now is acknowledged, in part at least, that we are far more plastic and capable of being psychologically shaped by our experiences.[14] This literature further deconstructs the old idea of "the homosexual" and arrives at a more varied understanding of homosexual experience and behavior.

Coincidentally, the homosexual type may have disappeared, but the heterosexual type has not. Well over 90 percent of the population are found in this category and have heterosexual-only attraction and experience. There is, thus, some justification for calling this natural, with a small "n."

## The Historical Culture of Gender Relationships and Homosexuality

Any approach that focuses on homosexuality without seeing the fuller family, gender, marriage and sexual patterns that shape a culture is flawed. The assumption often is made that there is a certain proportion of the population that is homosexual in most cultures. The level of disclosure may vary, but the proportion stays roughly the same. But what if the proportion of homosexual relationships varies depending on the culture and prevailing attitudes?

According to the ancient Greeks, men were heroes, warriors, thinkers and rulers, while women were for childbearing and domestic duties. Men were identified with culture and the polis, the ordering of human affairs, which is what lifts us above the animal. Men had two kinds of sexual relationship: That with women was procreational and functional, while that between men was nobler and more sublime. Theirs was an elitist male-adulating culture of which homosexuality was part andwhich left a subsidiary and residual role for sexual relationships with women. In Athens, Sparta and elsewhere, the culture unusually was affirming of homosexual activity.

Roman culture was more conservative and family-centered in a conventional sense, except when influenced by Greek culture, and much of the period up to the Renaissance was deeply influenced by Christianity. During this time, as far as the evidence allows us to see, homosexuality seems to have been more marginal. But the Renaissance saw the return of the glorification of the male in a similar way to the Greeks. Renaissance Man was center stage in terms of his art, power, mind and achievements. Along with this there was some rekindling of homosexual relationships (as Shakespeare's early sonnets show), but it should not be overstated.

This also was an era when competition between the sexes began to develop. Man and woman were idealized and cross-gender relationships assumed a greater complexity.

In the 17th and 18th centuries, Christian heterosexual idioms dominated, although by the early 19th century these had found expression in the idea of Romantic Love, which sometimes was extra-marital.

There was, however, a substantial change in the middle and late 19th century. Victorian sexual mores demanded a greater distance between men and women because of the dangers of loose sexual encounters. Even more important was the growth of male-only associations and organizations. The army, navy, clergy, universities and government long had been male-dominated, but to them were added the Civil Service, businesses, professions, clubs and many other groups.

Moreover, this pattern was pushed back into younger age

groups with male public schools, Sunday schools and other youth groups like Cubs and Scouts. Segregation also was present in many working-class communities with male workplaces, pubs, sports and hobbies. Women's culture was home, children, extended family and housework.

Part of the male culture included homosexuality. The middle class pattern often involved quite an early separation from both father and mother, and was accompanied by a situation where boys came to sexual maturity when in contact only with members of their own sex.

This cultural milieu existed alongside a Christian moral culture, which declined rapidly in influence with the advent of largely secular television after the middle of the 20th century.

With this decline, homosexuality gradually became more publicly acknowledged.

At the same time, women moved into university education and the professions. Schools and many other single-sex institutions became co-educational.

The segregation of genders decreased and became less possible with the growth of independent youth cultures. Some institutions were slow to change but, by the 1960s, substantial desegregation had occurred, especially among the young.

## Gay Recruitment and the Breakdown of the Heterosexual Family

During the 1970s and 1980s, homosexuality became publicly acknowledged and the moral culture became more strongly liberal, championing the freedom of each individual to pursue the sexual relationship of their choice.

Gay groups campaigned for the right to be publicly recognized on the same basis as heterosexuals and to invite others to practice a homosexual lifestyle. People were invited to "come out" and publicly acknowledge their homosexuality, thereby slaying the weight of social judgment and socially-induced guilt.

There also was a pattern of community development where gays tended to congregate in certain areas of major cities like New York, London and San Francisco – both because these offered a haven from external disapproval and also because it was easier to follow a homosexual lifestyle there.

Thus, during this era there was both an advocacy of homosexuality as natural and as something which needed to be acknowledged publicly.

This change did not occur in isolation. There was a far wider upheaval in heterosexual relationships. This included a liberal embracing of freedom in pre- and extramarital relationships, an increasing number of women moving into previously all-male educational institutions and workplaces, and a curtailing of family size through contraception and abortion.

> The perspective evident in the Hebrew and Christian Scriptures involves an understanding of the creation of man and woman as a purposive act so they could live in communion with one another, in wider relationships, but especially in monogamous marriage.

One undoubted outcome of these changes, especially when linked to the easier availability of divorce, was a widespread breakdown in marriages and families. The scale was considerable, rising to 4 in 10 marriages and families. This marked a momentous social change. Now, a generation is approaching marriageable age having, in many cases, witnessed the failure of their parents' marriage. They often, at least temporarily, are opting for cohabitation rather than marriage. Thus, there is a widespread awareness of failure and crisis in heterosexual relationships, and probably more serious patterns of parental (usually father) loss experienced by many children. It is not difficult to see how this could throw into doubt the gender and sex experiences of many children of both sexes.

There also is a power battle between the sexes marked by distrust and alienation. In an earlier era there was enforced gender distance, but now the withdrawal is voluntary. Women experiencing the absence of their fathers, sexual harassment, rape, violence and neglect can have deep misgivings about relationships with men. Men encountering independent, powerful women for the first time suddenly can find themselves vulnerable and unsure about commitment. The quality of this alienation between the sexes, therefore, is very different and post-liberal in the sense that the fruits of freedom have been tasted and they often are bitter and sexually destructive.

It is not just heterosexual relationships that have moved on from the liberalism of the 1970s and 1980s. A big impact was made by the HIV/AIDS crisis, which confronted the homosexual community with the fact that the actions of some of its members, initially inadvertently and later consciously, were risking the lives of other community members.

At that time, the community began to construct norms for sexual activity. The liberal norm of casual sexual encounters no longer was viable as it became clear how damaging these encounters could be. As a result, the longer term quality of relationships became just as much an issue as it was becoming within the heterosexual community.

This brief survey suggests the following: First, the social construction of heterosexuality and homosexuality changes and differs. Second, a range of social influences – peers, schools, gender culture, recruitment – may be influential in the development of homosexuality. Third, as every gay person knows, much homosexual experience has been shaped and complicated by the reactions of others. Fourth, we now have a gay community with its own ideological responses and stances.

## 'Coming Out' and Some Possible Gay Mistakes

Relatively recently, the gay movement has adopted a policy

toward the dominant culture. First, in the face of long-term public disapproval, it has asked members of its community to "come out" and declare their sexual identity. The aim of this policy clearly is to challenge orthodoxy, to brave condemnatory attitudes and to develop communal solidarity. It is a very understandable reaction.

Yet, this philosophy is based on the idea that gays should embrace the Naturalism that has labeled them in the first place. Coming out is to declare oneself homosexual. There are a number of levels at which this may not be accurate and, therefore, is likely to create problems.

I would not think of announcing to anyone, "I am heterosexual." This is not only because mine is the more common pattern of sexual experience, but also because it is not the defining characteristic of my life. More important than my sexuality is my relationship with God, my wife, children, work, thoughts, feelings and experiences.

The problem with "being gay" is that the label tends to dominate, becoming a fixation that closes down the possibilities of relationships and life. This may create personal crises – the overwhelming sense of "being gay" some have felt, and the aggression associated with "coming out."

A Naturalistic definition of homosexuality also creates or, more accurately, perpetuates divisiveness and hostility by heightening the differences between homosexuals and heterosexuals. Jason Annetts and Bill Thompson make the point well, pointing out that the *Gay Times* stirred fear of homophobia by identifying 48 murders of gay men over four years when, actually, this was an under-representation of their numbers in the community as a whole. They also note that the portrayal of Christian attitudes often is inaccurate. The group that was supposed to be unrelentingly hostile had established the first AIDS hospice in Europe.[15]

There is another, more personal, problem. There are many people who have been told, after a same-sex experience, that they are gay or lesbian. Their self-understanding thereby is locked into a frame of reference that identifies themselves as homosexuals, when they merely have had a homosexual encounter. Indeed, it is possible for a sexual partner using coercion or persuasion to argue on the basis of homosexual experience where some arousal has occurred that a person is gay. It is a way of trapping a person into a relationship and, because we have strong sexual memories, it may become a self-fulfilling prophecy. Especially if this occurs with a young person, it will be the source of great pain and distress.

Of course, there are many who have not gone this route but, for those who have, the result is to create an idea of a fixed sexual identity that only is true insofar as they believe it of themselves. If this way of arguing is used manipulatively, it is clearly wrong. Yet, the gay lobby is using quite coercive measures like "outing" to persuade people to adopt a label of gay identity on the basis of a homosexual experience.

This also may contribute toward homophobia. Those who have had some homosexual attraction, often when they are young, will react against a label that does not fit them with some vehemence because they do not want to be trapped in this all-encompassing identity.

## A Social Analysis of Homosexual Orientation

It appears likely that the development of lesbian relationships partially may be rooted in the suffering that has occurred in heterosexual cohabitation and marriage relationships, especially during the period of breakdown. Abuse, rape, unfaithfulness and neglect have left many women despairing of the opposite sex and moving into more dependable relationships with other women.

Often, the directing principle of these changes has been relational, rather than sexual. What they highlight is the alienation between the sexes. Other lesbian relationships are matters of open choice in the face of a number of sexual options.

Men have a different pattern. Some homosexual experience has to do with the long-term significance of male culture and gender segregation in institutions, especially schools and colleges. Cultures where high levels of segregation between the sexes occur tend to generate homosexual cultures. With many boys coming to sexual maturity at a time when most of their close relationships are male, it is likely that some of them would experience and come to identify themselves with male-male sexuality. This pattern has two forms. One involves peer interaction; the other involves young boys being initiated into homosexual relations by older men. The latter is a more sinister pattern, though no more so than in heterosexual relationships. There clearly is a need to eradicate all patterns of older people abusing the weakness and immaturity of children and young people to fulfill their own sexual desires.

There are many different routes to homosexual experience and we have considered some of them – same-sex cultures, initiation by peers and elders, arousal that is identified with men, fear or disgust with women and psychological reactions that are male-identity rejecting or woman fearing.

There also is a strong relational theory for which there now is substantial evidence. Children should grow up with the affirmation, support, love and respect of two parents. This is not just an assertion, but reflects a basic created human need. Each parent is important, and we begin with the relationship with the father. When boys find, or feel, that their father is absent, they experience a lack of love and a deep emotional repudiation of who they are. This gives them what often is called "father-hunger," a deep need that cannot be met because of the rupture in the relationship with the father. The consequence is a search for a same-sex bond that will tend to be sexual, but which does not have at its heart a sexual focus or need. It easily can develop a homosexual or promiscuous focus, but that is not its real meaning. Only when the issue is addressed in terms of the deep non-sexual love, which involves our relationship with God and our parents, can the deepest need be met.

Young men often receive very negative pictures of the intimate relationships between men and women. Many of them have seen their mother leave their father because she often initiates the divorce. The fear and lack of confidence in relating properly to women often is strong. Second, many boys have remained with their mother and faced an absent father. The loyalty to her and her situation and the pain associated with the broken marriage may leave a legacy difficult for the son to overcome. It remains an unresolved part of lives that often can be carried for decades.

The relationship with the mother similarly is significant. First, if the mother's relationship with the father is domineering and judgmental, or if the father fails in his relationship with the mother, then quite clearly the son can grow up with severe doubts about his ability to relate well with a woman. Either women are perceived as a threat or there is an internal sense of likely failure. These fears and responses run deep because they are generated, sometimes without foundation, early in life. They often are there well before puberty, so that either the longing for a father finds expression in homosexual longing or the fear of heterosexual relationships is resolved by involvement in homosexual ones.

> Any resentment felt by those who want their relationships affirmed comes in part from the different focus for living given by the Christian faith as opposed to current individualist attitudes. The latter focuses directly on what is good for me, and then works from that to a range of subsidiary conclusions.

This explanation, as one important social dynamic engendering homosexual relations, long has been observed and has widespread support as an explanation.[16] Schofield's 1965 study, for example, looked at three homosexual groups. A third came from disrupted homes, usually with the father killed in the war or absent after divorce, and another 38 percent had poor relations with their father.[17]

This understanding offers a number of insights. First, it may explain why male homosexual experience appears to be more prevalent than lesbian experience. Mothers are far less often absent, withdrawn and hostile to their children than are fathers. By war, death, divorce and occupational pressure, men have been less present. There often is an unmet need for men to love and be loved, which explains why for many the quest is not primarily or even significantly sexual. The sex may just be a trade-off for affection. Thus, much in the formation of homosexual attraction and experience may well be father replacement.

It would be understandable for members of the gay community to feel that it is just another way of labeling homosexual experience as pathological and this is another form of homophobia. The point repeatedly needs to be made that this explanation may not be true in every case. If it is true in a substantial number of cases that homosexual relations are symptomatic of an earlier formative cause, however, then that needs to be acknowledged. There is a relatively easy way to find out. We have in Britain a situation now where 20 percent of families with dependent children are headed by a lone mother[18] and roughly 80,000 boys annually experience family breakdown, usually with the loss of their father.[19] If the above analysis is correct, this is generating problems for young men on a scale that already is considerable and cannot escape public notice much longer.

Of course, many gay people will deny that their sexual experience is pathological in one of the ways suggested here. They also will argue rightly that much of the pathology of gay sexuality has been created by homophobic patterns, social and medical fears, and the labeling of homosexuality as immoral. This certainly is the case and needs to be acknowledged. Secrecy, persecution and public abuse have been part of the experience of the gay community. Clearly, part of the purpose of "coming out" is to escape these experiences.

Another area of concern is whether the choice of homosexual partners has anything to do with fear of women, either in general or particularly sexual. The answer to this question probably is ambivalent. In many cases, there is no fear. Indeed, man-woman friendships become easier for women when the attitude of the predatory male is removed and when male machismo is not part of the relationship. Where segregation of men and women occurs or where women use power in sexual and other terms in relationships, however, there can be a retreat from cross-gender intimacy. This obviously is important in some lesbian relationships where abuse, cruelty and inhumanity have led women to find care and respect with one another.

In individualist terms, each person is free to define relationships according to their own wishes and inclinations. There are no permanent norms defining relationships. In earlier times, homosexual relationships were felt to be wrong, but little attempt was made to explain why. They were merely a taboo that everybody was expected to observe. Now, people are asking why not a homosexual relationship if it suits me, and answers are not forthcoming. Not surprisingly, therefore, those who are considering such a relationship are more likely to proceed.

## Biblical and Christian Responses

The orthodox Christian understanding is that homosexual relationships are wrong and, although there are attempts to modify or reinterpret this understanding, this meaning of the biblical texts stands up to good scholarly interpretation.[20] It is important to understand the fuller biblical context in which judgments against homosexual activity are made.

The perspective evident in the Hebrew and Christian Scriptures involves an understanding of the creation of man

and woman as a purposive act so they could live in communion with one another, in wider relationships, but especially in
monogamous marriage. The underlying commitment to the
mutuality of male and female works against gender segregation in marriage, family and the wider society.

In this view, same-sex friendships are good but homosexuality, adultery, incest and pre-marital sex harm relationships.
Those who accept this view expect norms of sexual relationships to be part of the discipline of the community and view
homosexual practices as opposed to God's basic precepts for
human life.

In Leviticus 20, homosexuality is forbidden along with a
range of other activities relating to family life and gender:
sacrificing children, disrespecting father and mother, engaging in incest, committing adultery, having intercourse with a
woman during her period, and bestiality. It is clear that these
commands are laying down basic structural principles for
marital, sexual and family relationships. Thus, for example,
to have sex with a member of one's family is to compromise
that family relationship and other members of the family. To
marry a woman and her mother puts each in an untenable
position and invites tragedy.

The commands are intended to rule relationships for the
children of Israel, but reflect a structural principle that man is
made for woman and woman for man, as laid out in the great
creation narrative of Genesis 2. This is not just a physiological or sexual relationship, but a fully personal man-woman
relationship that is contravened by homosexual relationships.

Romans 1 addresses a different level of concern. It focuses
on what happens in human cultures when God worship,
which establishes the right basis for human relationships, is
replaced by worship of nature (v. 23) and human creatures (v.
25). Here, idolatry results in distorted relationships, and Paul
refers to what are obviously patterns of cult prostitution and
promiscuous homosexuality. This text, however, cannot be
dismissed as focusing only on homosexual promiscuity for

the clear meaning of the text is that the character of the relationship is wrong. This is echoed in other texts, like I Corinthians 6:9-10 and I Timothy 1:9-10. Here, we must ask what Paul's point of appeal is.

> For this reason God gave them up to dishonorable passions. Their women exchanged natural relations for unnatural, and the men likewise gave up natural relations with women and were consumed in passion for one another, men committing shameless acts with men and receiving in their own persons the due penalty for their error (Rom. 1:26-7).

Paul appeals here to what is natural. The structure of the argument is that because people have lost touch with God, they also have lost touch with the created, natural and good meaning of relationships. This is different from the Naturalism we looked at earlier where the idea of autonomous Human Nature led to a quest for the innate identity of the homosexual. Paul assumes the normativity of faithful marital relationships as the locus for genital sex.

Paul's focus, and that of the Bible elsewhere, also is on lust. This is both a heterosexual and homosexual problem, in and outside of marriage. Lust destroys relationships; it involves wrong attitudes; it dissociates love and sex; and it harms a person's relationship with God because it exalts the ego above all else. In our culture, lust often is reinterpreted as erotica, arousal or sexual expression, and it is justified through a variety of self-pleading arguments. Yet, lust hurts and damages people through rape, abuse and impersonal sex on a scale that validates the biblical analysis. The self-passion of lust, which often is loveless while declaring its love, is a universal human problem. Homosexual activity also often is prompted by lust and sexual gratification. Cory (1951) argues that because men traditionally are more predatory, male-male relationships are likely to be more promiscuous and self-gratifying, but this is, as we have seen, a limited cultural judgment.

Paul, in I Corinthians 6:9-11, says:

> Do not be deceived: Neither the sexually immoral, not idolaters, nor adulterers, nor male prostitutes, nor homosexual offenders, nor thieves, nor the greedy, nor drunkards, nor slanderers, nor swindlers will inherit the Kingdom of God. And that is what some of you were. But you were washed, you were sanctified, you were justified in the name of the Lord Jesus Christ and by the Spirit of our God.

Clearly, Paul is saying that we mustn't think we can be Christians without righteous living, and the unacceptable characteristics he focuses on are self-indulgence and lust. Lust uses another person and desanctifies the inner bond of love. Sinful desires and lusts stand alongside adultery, envy, malice, murder and gossip, all of which may be disastrous to our lives.

Is it possible to have truthful gay relationships, which are not marked by lust but by mutual love and care?

Clearly, in these relationships there can be love, faithfulness and many of the other aspects of friendship so highly praised in the Bible. The fun, acceptance and trust of friendship are good and should not be gainsaid. Indeed, the depth of friendship and its near central place in human life need to be recaptured. One of the most important truths of Christianity is that we are friends of Jesus and love one another as friends (John 15:12-17). Same-sex friendships are good for everybody, as well as cross-gender friendships.

Even a loving and truthful practicing homosexual relationship, however, rules out the union of man and woman in marriage, the sexual union of marriage, the procreation of children and the sharing of parenting as mother and father. There is a lack of marital wholeness before God. These are losses and, if the real meaning of sexual activity is as an expression of marital love, there also is a sense in which homosexual activity is untrue to its purpose. Whatever its subjective meaning, it does not dwell in these great themes of human existence.

We are asking whether something is wrong within an immediate relationship, but there is an even bigger picture. Humankind was created both male and female. They are intended to help one another. The two genders are opened to one another to rediscover the fullness of humanity, neither man nor woman, but both together. What is being upheld here is not just heterosexuality, although physiology and the pattern of progeny show the created purpose of the human body in relation to one another, but the structure of human relationships. The unity of the marriage bond, the shared two-gender pattern of parenting, and the cooperation of men and women in all areas of life provide structures that are good to live in.

Admittedly, that is not the immediate experience of many people, including those who opt for lesbian and gay lifestyles, and individualism in our culture tends to invite people to consider only their own ego-centered relationships. But the Bible has a bigger perspective of God-given structures for living, of how we are meant to live in those structures in love, faithfulness and tenderness. The route through problems in marriage and gender relationships is not to throw out the structures, but to recognize the failures and hurt that have occurred and reclaim what is good through repentance and openness to God. Thus, homosexuality is, in Christian terms, a breakdown in the gender structure of relationships in which we are expected to live good lives.

Any resentment felt by those who want their relationships affirmed comes in part from the different focus for living given by the Christian faith as opposed to current individualist attitudes. The latter focuses directly on what is good for me, and then works from that to a range of subsidiary conclusions. Thus, from this particular vantage point, sexual needs can be met in homo- and heterosexual ways and there is no necessary distinction between them.

The Christian focus, however, is on obedience to God, which involves a whole range of prohibitions, including the

Ten Commandments and others we have examined. To many in our culture, these prohibitions seem irksome. Even many Christians chafe at times. But the Christian understanding is that what is true and good may be found in God's revelation to us and especially through the life and teaching of Christ. Thus, Christians believe that the central point is not doing it "our way," but in God's way and on God's terms.

## A Re-evaluation

In summary, then, Christians who distinguish between homosexual nature and homosexual practice as a basis for understanding what a Christian response to homosexuality should be probably are not thinking clearly. Talking about "homosexuals" is less than helpful, first because identity does not rest in one's sexuality, but in our full human relationship with God; and second because few people unequivocally are "homosexual."

The cultural idiom that males are "men" or else they are gay, together with the tendency to identify people as either "homosexual" or "straight," has created and encouraged much homophobia. Both positions are wrong. This and the false fears about sexual identity among those with some homosexual attraction or experience need to be acknowledged in the wider community. There is a problem, especially for the young, of assuming that some homosexual attraction or experience means that they are homosexual by nature. The underlying concept is flawed, the experience probably is trivial, and the emphasis of the gay community on instant self-identification is misleading. The gay movement's emphasis on "coming out" may be problematic, first, in not accurately stating what is going on in people's lives where bisexual experience overwhelmingly is common, and because sexual identity is a fixated idea. It also encourages stereotyping and breaks down the community relations that should exist across the gay/straight barrier.

The Christian opposition to homosexual relationships needs

to be carefully defined. In part, it is opposition to patterns of lust and self-gratification, which occur similarly in heterosexual relationships. These relationships use and degrade others. It also is because of the Christian belief that marriage is the unique universal structure for sexual relationships allowing union, procreation and two-sex parenting of children.

Clearly, this is at odds with some gay interpretations of relationships. Within the church, dealing with this tension must involve a Christian sharing in community, a respect for each person, a refusal to label and stereotype, and a loving response to the problems carried from early life.

*Dr. Alan Storkey is dean of Postgraduate Studies at Oak Hill College, London. He holds degrees and teaches in the disciplines of sociology, economics and philosophy, and serves as chair of the Movement for Christian Democracy. This is a draft paper.*

## Endnotes

1.  Greenberg 1988, pp. 26-29, 67-68. David F. Greenberg, *The Construction of Homosexuality*. (Chicago: University of Chicago Press, 1988), p. 196.

2.  Greenberg, p. 417.

3.  Greenberg, pp. 350-351.

4.  Wellings, Kate et al. *Sexual Behaviour in Britain: The National Survey of Sexual Attitudes and Lifestyles*. (Harmondsworth: Penguin, 1994).

5.  *Ibid.*, p. 181.

6.  *Ibid.*, p. 187.

7.  *Ibid.*, p. 211.

8.  *Ibid.*, p. 181.

9.  *Ibid.*, p. 213.

10. *Ibid.*, p. 204.

11. *Ibid.*, p. 214, using a weighted mean of number of partners)

12. A key early paper was "The Homosexual Role" (1968) written by Mary McIntosh shortly after *The Wolfenden Report* (1967) which was the classic statement of the Naturalistic argument.

13. Jeffrey Weeks in his study, *Coming Out: Homosexual politics in Britain from the nineteenth century to the present* (1977) further explores social constructionism. *The Making of the Modern Homosexual* (ed Plummer 1981) persistently aims to debunk the category of "homosexual." Celia Kitzinger's study, *The Social Construction of Lesbianism* (1987), emphasizes that this was a movement opposed to patriarchy rather than a type of person.

14. Kitzinger in Angelli and Patterson 1995, pp. 136-61.

15. Plummer 1992, pp. 231-232.

16. See Jonas (1944), Henry (1950), Kolb and Johnson (1955), Allen (1958), West (1959), Bell (1981) and Moberley (1983).

17. Schofield 23-6, 77-9, 104-6.

18. *Social Trends* 1995, p. 34.

19. *Social Trends* 1995, p. 37.

20. Stott 1990, pp. 336-64.

# CHAPTER 6

# The Case for Heterosexual Marriage

## Mary Stewart Van Leeuwen

*C* *an I offer good reasons, as a social scientist, to*
*privilege stable heterosexual marriages over*
*the contemporary plurality of household forms to*
*which my own family bears witness? Or like North*
*Americans' gradual acceptance and even celebration of*
*cultural pluralism, should we regard the rise of premar-*
*ital cohabitation, serial monogamy, single childbearing*
*and gay parenting as the triumph of personal and gen-*
*erational choice over arbitrary – or at least outdated –*
*social patterns? My own position is that there, indeed,*
*are good empirical reasons both to privilege and*
*strengthen stable, heterosexual marriages.*

One of the mixed blessings of growing older is the experience of watching a younger generation of family members
grow from birth to adulthood. By "younger generation," I
mean not just my own children, but nieces, nephews, cousins
and the children of cousins. Some of these lives I have been
able to track at closer range than others. But with the help of
Christmas newsletters, e-mail and intermittent family

reunions at weddings, funerals and summer cottages, I keep abreast of the main events in the lives of many relatives and their adult children.

Family gatherings also prompt reminiscences about past generations – experiences with common parents, grandparents, aunts and uncles, many of whom have now died and all of whom grew to adulthood in a very different world from that of the late 20th century.

After a recent extended-family gathering at a summer cottage I began to think about generational differences in family crises. In my grandparents' and parents' generations, divorce virtually was unheard of – although family disruption and impoverishment due to the untimely death or illness of a spouse was not uncommon, and there is evidence that what used to be called "shotgun weddings" took place on both sides of my family. It was my own generation that began to partake of the divorce culture with a vengeance and, over the years, my husband and I have watched with distress as the marriages of various relatives in both our families have disintegrated.

Moreover, the divorces took place at progressively earlier stages as we moved from the 1960s to the 1980s. Divorcing couples closer to my parents' generation tended to separate when their children were in mid- to late adolescence; but my younger cousins and in-laws have divorced – sometimes more than once – at the stage when they had young children or none at all. In a couple of cases, the complications of child custody have caused a niece or nephew to drop almost completely off the family radar screen. Children I met in infancy, and whose baby pictures still sit in photo albums with those of my sons, went with their separated mothers – and, sometimes, a new stepfather – to a distant place, never to be seen (or, in one case, heard from) again.

Now, in the 1990s, I watch as a new generation of my family grows to adulthood. The daughters of two different cousins concluded they were lesbians and have entered into same-sex partnerships, one involving three children from her partner's previous marriage. The son-in-law of another cousin likewise decided that he was gay, and recently left his wife and children to live with a male lover. The cycle of divorce continues, particularly among the children of couples who themselves divorced when their children were still of school age. And among "Generation X" relatives, cohabitation and/or out-of-wedlock births have occurred not infrequently.

Let me acknowledge that there were understandable reasons for certain divorces and family members, including myself, often regarded these as the lesser of two evils. I also should add that both my husband and I come from fairly large extended families in which stable marriages still are more common than the patterns I have just been describing. But even if they weren't, would it matter? That is the question I am addressing in this essay. Can I offer good reasons, as a social scientist, to privilege stable heterosexual marriages over the contemporary plurality of household forms to which my own family bears witness? Or like North Americans' gradual acceptance and even celebration of cultural pluralism, should we regard the rise of premarital cohabitation, serial monogamy, single childbearing and gay parenting as the triumph of personal and generational choice over arbitrary – or at least outdated – social patterns?[1]

Many social scientists would answer that last question in the affirmative. Thus, wrote sociologist Judith Stacey in 1990, "In the postmodern period a truly democratic kinship order, one that does not favor authority, heterosexuality, a particular division of labor, or a single household or parenting arrangement [has become] thinkable for the first time in history."[2] Psychologist Diane Ehrensaft, writing in the late 1980s, concurred:

> It is imperative that mothering, the daily acts, concerns and sensibilities that go into the nurturance and rearing of a child, does not become obsolete, but that society makes room for mothering to extend to any combination of adults – women and men, women and women, or men

and men – who are committed to raising a child together. In other words, it is time for mothering to become a genderless affair.[3]

## Three Theological Qualifiers

My own position is that there, indeed, are good empirical reasons both to privilege and strengthen stable, heterosexual marriages. But before I present them, I want to make three assertions as a specifically Christian social scientist about what I am not defending.

First of all, I am a fifty-something psychologist who both has supported and benefited from the second wave of feminism since it burst onto the scene during my graduate school days in the 1960s. Without doubt, the changes wrought by feminism have enabled my husband and myself to combine academic careers with parenting in ways that would have been unthinkable even a quarter century ago. I mention this to make it clear that my defense of heterosexual co-parenting is not to be equated with a defense of the so-called "traditional" family in which paternal dominance, female economic dependence and a rigidly-gendered division of labor are taken as normative.

### *The Cultural Mandate vs. the Doctrine of Separate Spheres*

In fact, if I had to identify one issue on which all feminists – Christian or otherwise – are likely to agree, it would be the need to challenge what has been known for several generations as "the doctrine of separate spheres." This was the belief, developed in the wake of 19th century urbanization and industrialization, that by nature, divine mandate or both, men essentially were fitted for the public sphere: the academy, the marketplace and the political forum. Women, by contrast, were said to be uniquely fitted for those tasks (and, generally, *only* those tasks) associated with domesticity and child rearing. These they were to carry out in a state of economic and legal dependence on their husbands or related adult males.[4]

The resulting family form, which remained the societal ideal up through the 1950s, often (ironically) is known as the "traditional" family. Ironic because, in the long sweep of history, the truly traditional family is one in which workplace, dwelling space and child-rearing space coincide for both husbands and wives (think of your ancestors who ran family farms, or family businesses with living quarters above or behind the shop). Ironic, too, because even at the height of its acceptance, many people – especially rural, poor and working class people – could not even afford to buy into the single male-breadwinner model represented by the doctrine of separate spheres.

But from a Christian point of view, the doctrine of separate spheres has an even deeper problem. For when we look at what Reformed theologians call "the cultural mandate" of Genesis 1:26-28,[5] we do not find God saying to the first female, "Be fruitful and multiply," and to the first male "Subdue the earth." Both mandates are given to both members of the primal pair. Both are called to accountable dominion, sociability and responsible procreation. Made jointly in the image of God, both women and men are called to unfold the potential of creation in all areas of life. Together, they are to work out God's call to stewardship, justice and fidelity in ways that are sensitive to different settings and times in history and to the life cycle of male and female human beings.

Thus, any construction of gender relations involving an exaggerated or inflexible separation of the cultural mandate by sex is bound to run into trouble eventually because it is creationally distorted and, therefore, potentially unjust toward both sexes. The cultural mandate is a human – not a gendered – mandate.

### *Marriage: Part of Creation, But Fallen*

My first comment concerned the significance of the doctrine of creation for family relations. My second concerns what we might call "the fallout of the fall." Marriage is part of God's creation order. That it was meant to be a lifelong, "one flesh" monogamous union is affirmed in the creation accounts and reaffirmed by Jesus (e.g., Mark 10; Matt. 19; Luke 16) and the Pauline epistles (e.g., I Cor. 5 & 7; Eph. 5; I Tim. 3; Titus 1).

The gospels and epistles also make it clear that people need not marry in order to carry out the cultural mandate in cooperation with others, and Protestant Christians especially tend to forget this. Nevertheless, marriage is part of what God has approved for human life on earth, reflecting the unity-in-diversity of Father, Son and Holy Spirit, and the intended means by which future imagers of God are procreated.

Like all creation structures peopled by fallen human beings, however, marriage and family are the potential locus of much sin. As Christians strive to affirm the committed, heterosexual, two-parent family, they often are tempted to romanticize it as a "holy refuge" or a "haven in a heartless world." But the biblical record is full of accounts that tell us otherwise – records of the family feuds and sexual weaknesses of a host of Old Testament and New Testament notables. And today, as a member of my own denomination's recent Synodical Committee on Abuse, I can affirm that the prevalence rates of physical, psychological and sexual abuse in churched families pretty much are the same as in the population at large.[6]

Theologically speaking, families – even intact, two-parent Christian families – most accurately are likened to the little girl of nursery rhyme fame: when they're good, they're very, very good, and when they're bad, they're horrid. So, I am not defending a romanticized view of heterosexual marriage. Marriage, like all human relationships, requires hard work, self-insight and a willingness to listen, forgive and grow. It also needs the social support of family, friends and mentors, especially those who have wisdom, experience and a well-developed Christian worldview.[7]

## The Family of God is the First Family

My final qualifier has to do with what has been called "the new biologism" in family studies.[8] Some social scientists and theologians wishing to reaffirm heterosexual parenting have begun to do so by appealing to an updated version of the "blood is thicker than water" argument. Drawing on theories of evolutionary psychology[9] and on natural theology,[10] these writers claim that human beings invest most heavily in their own biological children in order to assure the survival of their own genes. They will be, however, progressively less generous to others in proportion as they share fewer genes with them, and will be least altruistic to non-related people.[11] This, then, becomes an argument for re-instituting barriers against easy divorce and for strengthening parents' ties to their own children, regardless of their socioeconomic situation or the state of their relationship to each other.[12]

I do not want to discount the pull of biological ties as a motivation for emotional bonding and self-sacrifice. Indeed, the concern I expressed earlier for various members of my own family indicates that I share this motivation. And it surely is significant that God inaugurates the cosmic, biblical drama of history by choosing a particular people – the Jews – and calling them to follow him as a tribal people who are to take family ties and blood lines seriously.

Even in the Old Testament, however, God begins to relativize biological ties as our ultimate human loyalty. He includes foreigners such as Rahab and Ruth in Jesus' genealogy. He sends children like Isaac and John the Baptist to aging parents, contrary to normal expectation. And in Jesus' incarnation, God finally "sets aside ... the ordinary process of human reproduction to initiate the work which will undo the fall. 'The power of the most high' brings about this birth of the child that is 'set for the fall and rising of many in Israel' (Luke 1:35; 2:34)."[13]

Not just the manner of Jesus' coming, but his life and teachings underscore the fact that marriage and family now take a back seat to the universal proclamation of God's salvation and the formation of a new "first family." This is to be a worldwide kingdom-building company in which membership depends not on bloodlines, but on faith in the Messiah.[14] It surely is significant that members of the early church rescued exposed Roman infants and raised them in their own families as gifts from God and that ,in our own time, Christians foster and adopt children at higher rates than the population at large. Blood certainly is thicker than water, but for those who have responded to God's gift of grace, "the blood of the Lamb" is meant to be the thickest of all.

## Three Competing Views of Marriage

I have begun with some confessional assumptions about family life that I hold as a Christian working in the Reformed theological tradition. But, clearly, those assumptions are not shared by social scientists who work from other faith-based worldviews. What are these competing worldviews and how do they affect their adherents' view of marriage?

In his analysis of the Hawaii same-sex marriage debate, David Orgon Coolidge, a legal scholar at the Washington-based Ethics and Public Policy Center, has identified three contending models of marriage in current North American culture.[15]

The first, which he calls the Traditional or Complementarity Model, is closest to my own. It has been the basis of all Western family law until recently, and goes back to English common law and church canon law of the Middle Ages.[16] In this view, marriage is an *institution* – a whole that is more than just the sum of its parts, and a sexual community in which the nurture of children, by procreation or adoption, is a central function. It assumes that the universe has created order and purpose, not just materially but socially, and that sexual complementarity is part of this order. It sees marriage as the basic social institution through which men and women unite lives, establish families and form intergenerational bonds. It is a "sovereign sphere" that has its own integral character and is meant to work together with other institutions – such as commerce, science, education and the arts – to form a just and healthy society.[17]

In this view, marriage as part of the creation order pre-exists any definition of it by religion or the state. Marriage, however, may be blessed by religious institutions, either as a sacrament or a covenant, and should be legally recognized and protected by the state although, with due regard for the realities of human frailty, that may require pastoral or legal exceptions to this norm.

> During the 20th century in the U.S.A., the rate of divorce has risen tenfold, from 5 percent to almost 50 percent ... Many family studies scholars and professionals assume that this is an inevitable, if regrettable, result of living in an advanced industrial society and so we simply should learn to live with it.

The second model of marriage is rooted in liberal political theory that began to emerge during the 18th century Enlightenment period and, accordingly, Coolidge calls it the Liberal or Choice Model. In this view, marriage is not a social institution but simply a contract between individuals, the purpose of which is to maximize personal fulfillment, sexual and otherwise. It assumes a universe in which social order and obligation proceed not from creation norms, but from individual choice. It holds that rights are attached only "to free-floating individuals disconnected from their social context."[18]

Thus, in the Liberal Model the church may adhere privately to its own definition of marriage, but the secular state should treat it simply as a legal contract between equal individuals from which certain benefits (e.g., joint pensions and health care) will follow as long as that contract operates. Nowadays, of course, the contract is capable of easy legal dissolution whenever either of its parties ceases to feel individually fulfilled by it.

Moreover, in this model, child rearing is incidental rather than intrinsic to marriage. It is something marriage partners may or may not decide to add to their union and how or when they do this is not the business of either church or state. It is fair to say that, with the advent of no-fault divorce (which, in effect, also means *unilateral* divorce) the Liberal Model is on its way to replacing the Complementarity Model as the assumed legal and philosophical framework for marriage in our society.[19]

Coolidge finally points out that a third view of marriage also is emerging, which he calls the Postmodern or Commitment model. On first glance, it is easy to have sympathy for this view because it rejects the rugged individualism of the liberal model and recognizes human beings as social creatures who need stable relationships. Its adherents view marriage ideally as a lifelong interpersonal and sexual partnership. It is seen as a central institution – albeit a socially constructed one – whose purpose is to encourage intimate and enduring relationships that link couples and households to wider communities. But this view differs from the traditional model in *not* assuming that marriage is based on sexual complementarity. Rather, it is based on the right of all people to participate fully in the institutions of society and their accompanying benefits.

In the Postmodern view, it only is the *motivation* for being in a committed sexual relationship that matters; the sex of the people involved is irrelevant. Hence, the legal, cultural and religious benefits of marriage should be available to any people who wish to make such a commitment. Those endorsing the legalization of gay marriage in Hawaii often seem to assume a Postmodern model of marriage, as do those in mainline churches who support religious ceremonies for same-sex unions.

And some postmodern social scientists go even further. Consider the following comments by University of California sociologist Judith Stacey:

> [G]ranting full legal recognition to lesbian and gay relationships could have dramatic, and salutary consequences ... If we begin to value the meaning and quality of intimate bonds over their customary forms, people might devise marriage and kinship patterns to serve diverse needs ... For example, the "companionate marriage," a much celebrated but less often realized, ideal of modern sociological lore, could take on new life. Two friends might decide to "marry" without basing their bond on erotic or romantic attachment ... Or, more radical still, perhaps some might dare to question the dyadic limitations of Western marriage and seek some of the benefits of extended family life through small group marriages, arranged to share resources, nurturance and labor. After all, if it is true that the two-parent family is better than a single family, as family-values crusaders proclaim, might not three- four- or more-parent families be better yet, as many utopian communards have long believed?[20]

Clearly, Stacey's pluralistic vision of sex and marriage is just that – a speculative exercise based on her own postmodern worldview. And, as we have seen, worldviews and their accompanying models of marriage are faith-based and, therefore, not easily disputed. But most social scientists still claim to be empiricists, who will allow their biases to be challenged by the results of rigorously designed research.

So, when we look at research that might be said to test the Liberal and Postmodern models of marriage, what do we find? To begin with, I have said that our society's easy acceptance of no-fault divorce is a result of its acceptance of the Liberal model. What, then, do we find when we look at 30 years of research on the effects of divorce as a liberal institution?

## The Myth of the Good Divorce

During the 20th century in the U.S.A., the rate of divorce has risen tenfold, from 5 percent to almost 50 percent, with similar if less dramatic rises in other industrialized nations.[21] Many family studies scholars and professionals assume that this is an inevitable, if regrettable, result of living in an advanced industrial society and so we simply should learn to live with it. "[W]e should *institutionalize* divorce," writes Harvard sociologist William Goode, "accept it as we do other institutions and build adequate safeguards as well as social understandings and pressures to make it work reasonably well."[22] How did our culture arrive at such a casual – or, at least, resigned – view of broken marriages?

> Children of divorce on average show more antisocial behavior toward peers and adults, more depression and more learning problems than children from intact homes with two biological parents.

Until about 30 years ago, divorce largely was the activity of wealthy socialites, business magnates and movie stars, who used it as a calculated means of upward social or economic mobility. But despite their voyeuristic interest in the coupling and uncoupling of the rich and famous, most people – from academics and churchmen to women's magazine editors and leftist socialists – decried this kind of "instrumental divorce." It was seen as self-indulgent behavior that brought market values into an area of life – the family – that was meant to transcend such considerations.

Beginning in the late 1950s, however, what might be called "expressive divorce" became more and more the norm among the very classes that previously had decried instrumental divorce.[23] Mediated by no-fault divorce laws and by therapists, self-help books and other vehicles of popular culture, divorce came to be seen (by all but a perceived handful of religious reactionaries) as a positive growth experience. Through it, women would learn to be their own persons and children would benefit from lessened marital conflict and fresh relationships in the stepfamilies they might acquire. As Joseph Epstein put it in a 1974 book, "In some circles ... living out one's days within the confines of a single marriage might even be thought to show an insufficiency of imagination, evidence that one is possibly a bit callow emotionally."[24]

## The Effects of Divorce on Children

But over the last 20 years, social scientists have collected a lot of data on the fallout of divorce, including surveys and longitudinal studies of children affected by it. And, amazing as it might seem to a culture still caught up in the rhetoric of expressive divorce, *regardless of their place on the ideological or political spectrum*, social scientists now are agreed that divorce is anything but a minor blip on the developmental landscape. Children of divorce on average show more antisocial behavior toward peers and adults, more depression and more learning problems than children from intact homes with two biological parents. They are one-and-a-half to two-and-a-half times more likely to drop out of high school, to become teenage parents and to be neither in school nor the workforce as young adults. As older adults, they have less sense of psychological well-being, less marital satisfaction, heightened risk of divorce, and even a shorter life-span.[25]

Some skeptics question the assumption of a causal connection between divorce and these negative outcomes. They argue that it is not the absence of a parent, but simply post-divorce economic strain on single-parent families, that accounts for these results.

But other studies show the effects persist even when income is controlled, for example, when generous alimony is paid or when children's economic status is raised by the custodial parent's remarriage.[26]

At best, only half the variance associated with these problems can be attributed to the economic stresses that accompany single parenthood, important and troubling though these are.

Other skeptics argue that it is pre- and post-divorce parental conflict that explains children's problems, and that these would disappear if we could only teach adults how to make divorce more civilized and less acrimonious. But despite the rising number of self-help books and divorce-related professionals, there is little evidence that the "divorce culture" of the past 30 years has resulted in improved co-parenting among most separated mothers and fathers. On the contrary, persistent tensions regarding financial obligations, visitation schedules and relationships to new partners characterize even the most "civilized" divorces, with predictably negative effects on the children who are being shuttled back and forth between households.[27]

Perhaps most significantly, another body of research shows that the negative effects of divorce also are common in children of single parents who never married and, thus, had no marital conflict to contend with.[28] So, clearly, there is something about *intact, two-parent* families that matters. Reasonably harmonious and mature parents support and spell each other off in child care. They are a constant presence in the child's life and, thus, can adjust to developmental changes and supply consistent moral guidance. They provide a backdrop of day-to-day predictability that allows children to concentrate on age-appropriate tasks. Divorce changes all this for the worse, so much so that even researchers with an otherwise liberal mindset, like Berkeley sociologist Judith Wallerstein, draw conclusions such as the following:

> There is little that is reassuring about the condition of children of divorce [either] in single-parent or remarried homes ... We have learned over many years of experience that divorce is not the circumscribed crisis in the life

of adult and child that we anticipated.

It is emphatically not a single event but a long-lasting process of radically changing family relationships that begins in the failing marriage, continues through the often chaotic period of the marital rupture and its immediate aftermath, and extends even further, often over many years of disequilibrium.[29]

## The Effects of Divorce on Adults

In terms of the adults involved, it needs to be pointed out that divorce is not the panacea for unhappy marriages that many people glibly assumed it would be 30 years ago. A common argument back then was that, by allowing unhappy marriages to dissolve easily, divorce actually would strengthen marriage as an institution since enduring first marriages, by definition, would be happy and those remarrying after divorce would be more likely to find compatible life partners the second time around.

> Data from 1973 to 1993 shows that the predicted increase in reported marital quality did not occur, in spite of climbing divorce rates. Instead, there has been a modest but steady decline in the percentage of people reporting themselves to be in "very happy" marriages over that time period.

But again, two decades of research have undermined these assumptions. For example, we now know that second marriages are at even greater risk of being broken by divorce than first marriages.[30] Another body of research has challenged the assumption that the average quality of marriage logically would increase as divorce became more readily available. Data from 1973 to 1993 shows that the predicted increase in reported marital quality did not occur, in spite of climbing divorce rates.

Instead, there has been a modest but steady decline in the percentage of people reporting themselves to be in "very happy"
marriages over that time period.

Norval Glenn, the sociologist who collected this data,
shows that they also correlate with a steady weakening of the
ideal of marital permanence and a steady rise in individualistic and materialistic values in his American samples. He
believes these trends reflect our culture's acceptance of the
liberal view of marriage – i.e., that marriage solely is for personal gratification and,
therefore, that the slightest
dissatisfaction warrants its
dissolution. "The conse-
quences of this change for
children," he writes, "are
now widely recognized,
and those for adults, while
less severe, also seem to be
distinctly negative. An
increasingly hedonistic
form of marriage seems to be decreasingly able to facilitate
the hedonistic strivings of those who participate in it."[31]

> Family studies
> researchers across the
> ideological spectrum from
> left to right agree that
> lasting marriage, on the
> whole, is better for both
> children and adults.

## The Myth of the Bad Marriage

So, in a host of ways, divorce is not good for children or
their parents. But is marriage as an institution, on the whole,
any better for the adults involved?

Glenn's research on declining marital satisfaction might
seem to suggest not. In addition, there is an earlier research
literature suggesting that so-called traditional marriage is
more advantageous for men than for women. Among never-
married people, for example, the rate of mental illness is
higher for men than for women. But among married people,
the reverse is the case: women show a higher rate of symp-
toms than men.[32] Many people blame this discrepancy on the
doctrine of separate spheres, which often led to economic

dependency and social isolation for wives, while allowing husbands to function in the public sphere with the added advantage of a full-time helper at home.

This discrepancy, however, is beginning to disappear with the progressive dismantling of gendered separate spheres. More importantly, there is another large literature showing that, on the whole, marriage positively is associated with enhanced well-being in both women and men.[33] Using another data set that spanned 20 years, demographer Linda Waite recently compared the psychological, physical and economic health of married people with that of cohabiting couples, and with never-married and widowed people as well. After matching her samples in all other respects, she found that married men and women are at lower risk of dying at any age than never-married, divorced or widowed people. On average, they also have better health, more wealth and higher earnings (although it still is the case that married motherhood reduces women's time in the labor force and, thus, lowers their lifetime wages relative to their husbands). Finally, married people of both sexes report more physical and emotional satisfaction with their sex lives than either sexually-active single people or cohabiting couples.[34]

Again, it is fair to ask about the direction of causality in these data. Does marriage actually enhance people's well-being or is it just that more successful and healthier people have a better chance of getting married? Statistical analyses have shown that at least half the strength of these positive effects is due not to selectivity into marriage, but to something about marriage itself when it is "good enough," even if not perfect. Linda Waite suggests four factors:

First, the "till death do us part" aspect of a successful marriage helps partners to trust each other, to learn about and accommodate each other's tastes (sexual and otherwise) and to develop some skills while downplaying others that the spouse has in his or her repertoire.

Second, marriage involves not just a pooling of skills, but

of economic and social resources. This provides for spouses "a sort of small insurance pool against life's uncertainties, reducing their need to protect themselves – by themselves – from unexpected events."[35]

Third, in many ways married couples benefit from economies of scale – the "two can live about as cheaply as one" effect.

And, finally, marriage connects people to other family members, social groups and institutions (such as churches) that provide further support and – just as importantly – opportunities for service that help to give life meaning.

Obviously, cohabiting men and women also can benefit from things like economies of scale and pooling of resources. But Waite points out that cohabitation, by its very nature, does not imply a lifetime commitment, and cohabiting couples often have quite discrepant views about the future of their relationship. Often, the men are less committed to the relationship than their partners. Consequently, cohabitation is a particularly poor bargain for women – who, it must be recalled, also are the ones who can be left "holding the baby" if they happen to get pregnant.

Furthermore, cohabiting couples are much less likely than married people to pool economic resources; in many respects, they live as roommates who just happen to sleep together. And while marriage connects couples to other salient institutions, cohabitation appears to have the opposite effect: It often isolates couples from supportive and service-promoting groups.

## But Why *Heterosexual* Marriage?

I have just tested the liberal or "choice" model of marriage by examining the ongoing, negative effects of divorce on children and their parents and contrasting these with the overall positive effects of lasting marriages. Let me repeat that this literature no longer is controversial. Social scientists still differ as to whether high rates of divorce in our society are inevitable or reversible. In addition, no one denies that divorce may be a regrettable necessity in marriages plagued by chronic abuse, addiction, adultery or financial irresponsibility. But aside from these qualifiers, family studies researchers across the ideological spectrum from left to right agree that lasting marriage, on the whole, is better for both children and adults.

But we still have to test the third, Postmodern or Commitment, model of marriage. Recall that adherents of the Postmodern view enthusiastically support committed, lifelong partnerships and families, but reject the older notion that sexual complementarity is essential to marriage.

Among these are many self-identified gays and lesbians and "gay-positive" others who see no reason to limit either the benefits or responsibilities of marriage to heterosexual couples.[36] What is important in all families, they insist, is not "biological" but "social" parenting. By this they mean that whichever adults are responsible for the ongoing nurture of a child – and, hence, those to whom the child is attached – *are* the child's parents, regardless of where the sperm and egg came from that constituted the child's genetic origins and regardless of who bore the child.

Here I need to insert another qualifier. I already have said that social parenting is an important symbol and result of God's saving grace. The recognition that God's redeemed family is to come "from every tribe and nation" explains, in large part, why Christians have adopted children so consistently throughout history. But it is a big step from the norm of adopting children into a household organized around a married woman and man – or even a single adult who has ties to a larger extended family – to that of endorsing adoption or any other form of childbearing by same-sex parents. Confessional issues aside, do we have any *empirical* evidence that, as long as households stay stable, nurturant and economically viable, it does not matter for optimal development what combination of parents – male *and* female, males *or* females – a child has?

## *Research Limitations on Homosexual Parenting*

Since postmodern family forms are too recent to have seen many of their children grow to adulthood, this is a difficult question to answer. In a sense, it would be like trying to predict the effects of the divorce revolution on children before the first generation of divorced children grew up. In addition, other variables complicate any attempts to assess the impact of homosexual parenting.

A second very important question is the issue of sampling. It is comparatively easy to recruit samples of married and divorced individuals that adequately mirror the general population in terms of class and ethnicity but, since so many homosexuals still are closeted, representative sampling of their numbers still is not possible. Even gay-positive researchers acknowledge that the overwhelming amount of research on homosexuality has concentrated on individual, young, white, well-educated middle-class males. The fewer studies on domestic relationships also have concentrated on white, well-educated respondents.

Thirdly, by far the most common (and, therefore, the most commonly-studied) household form is that of formerly-married gay or lesbian parents – mostly the latter – who "came out" after divorce and secured at least shared custody of their children. These hardly are "pure cases" of homosexual parenting since the children were born into and spent the early formative years in a biological two-parent household.

Fourthly, of the smaller pool of homosexuals who have borne or adopted children outside of traditional marriage, the vast majority also are women. Thus, the pool of children growing up with gay *male* parents is far too small to constitute an adequate sample.

Finally, lesbian means for attaining parenthood are quite varied. Some resort to heterosexual intercourse; some seek anonymous sperm donations through women's health centers; some solicit the sperm of gay male friends. Some lesbian couples obtain sperm from a brother or male relative of one

woman and use it to impregnate the other, hoping to maximize the sense of biological connection both will have to the
child. Less common, because it is more complex and expen-
sive, is the route of fertilizing an egg from one woman with
donor sperm, then extracting and implanting it in the lover's
uterus. And because most adoption agencies do not allow
gay-couple adoptions (and, in America, some states still pro-
hibit it), independent adoption has been the most common
route to non-marital lesbian parenting in the past and still is
used by some today.[37]

## Premature Postmodern Optimism

Thus, many complications accompany attempts to assess
the outcome of homosexual parenting. There is the newness
of the phenomenon, the
fact that research strongly
is skewed toward mem-
bers of the white middle
class and toward post-
marriage lesbian parent-
ing, and the variety that
exists in the biological
and gestational histories
of non-marital children.[38]

> Any policy that discourages
> heterosexual co-parenting
> may undercut the feminist
> agenda by increasing male
> hostility to women and result-
> ing in the marginalization of
> women from public life.

None of this appears to have daunted the romantic view that
many postmodern family researchers have toward homosexual family forms. Indeed, one is reminded of the confident
way in which, 30 years ago and in the absence of supporting
research, other family theorists were heralding divorce as the
solution to every type of familial discontent.

Homosexual families are said to "exist and even thrive in a
society that stigmatizes them." They "break the mold of the
benchmark family by disturbing sexist and heterosexist
norms" with "relationships [that] offer a model of egalitarian
partnering and gender flexibility."[39]

As parents, they are "more nurturant and tolerant and their

children in turn more tolerant and empathetic, and less aggressive, than those reared by non-gay parents."[40]

All these claims are made despite the *acknowledged* impossibility of obtaining adequate samples that represent pure homosexual parenting, let alone homosexual parenting that matches the class, ethnic and educational diversity of the heterosexual families to which they so favorably are being compared.

Moreover, although most researchers have been at pains to point out that gay- and lesbian-reared children are no more likely to engage in homosexual experimentation than children in other kinds of families, some postmodern researchers openly and even enthusiastically suggest otherwise. Judith Stacey, reviewing a British study of the adult children of lesbian and non-lesbian women, notes with satisfaction that none of the latter, but a third of the former, reported having had either same-sex erotic experiences or a homosexual orientation.[41] With postmodern gusto, she affirms the influence of culture on sexual orientation and the liberated sexual flexibility this portends:

> Homophobes are quite correct to believe that environmental conditions incite or inhibit expressions of homosexual desire, no matter what its primary source ... This prospect should disturb only those whose antipathy to homosexuality derives from deeply held religious convictions or irrational prejudice. The rest of us could benefit from permission to explore and develop sexually free from the rigid prescriptions of what Adrienne Rich memorably termed "compulsory heterosexuality." Currently, lesbian and gay parents grant their children such permission much more generously than do other parents.[42]

All of this is to say that, for serious methodological reasons if for no other, the jury definitely is still out on the issue of how gay- and lesbian-raised children compare to those raised by two biological parents.

But are there other reasons to be doubtful about the wisdom of raising children in same-sex households? I think the answer is yes. To begin to explain this, we need to recall that the vast majority of such children are being raised in lesbian, not gay male, households. Analagously, the vast majority of the children of divorce are being raised by single-parent or remarried mothers, not fathers. Consequently, the relevant question for which we have data is: "How do children in general fare when *fathers* are absent – either physically or psychologically – from their children's lives, and what difference does their presence make?"

From my point of view, this is an important question because postmodern family researchers often assume that the pluralization of family forms to include lesbian (and, eventually, gay) couples raising children in no way will be incompatible with feminist concerns for justice toward women and girls. On the postmodern account, any agenda that undermines heterosexism automatically will undermine misogyny or sexism toward women, as well.[43] But as we shall see, this is not necessarily the case.

## Object Relations Theory: Defending Heterosexual Co-Parenting[44]

There is one set of feminist voices that hesitates to endorse an unlimited plurality of family forms, insisting instead on the necessity for strong involvement of both father- and mother-figures in child rearing. But far from trying to resurrect the so-called traditional family, with its doctrine of separate spheres, these feminist object-relations theorists argue that both male misogyny *and* the female impulse to over-invest in nurturing are rooted in the very gendering of the public/domestic split that feminists have worked to eradicate. On this account, any policy that discourages heterosexual co-parenting may undercut the feminist agenda by increasing male hostility to women and resulting in the marginalization of women from public life.[45]

## Father Absence as a Source of Misogyny

According to these feminists working in the depth-psycho-logical tradition, the problem begins in early infancy when children are highly bonded to a primary caretaker, who (in societies with a highly gendered division of labor) usually is a woman. That little girls, thus, have a same-sex caretaker as their primary love-object while little boys do not becomes significant around the age of three when children of both sexes acquire "gender constancy." This is the recognition that being male or female is a permanent state of nature and not affected by superficial changes in dress, grooming, behaviors, etc. Acquiring gender constancy is less immediately problematic for little girls, who can get a sense of security about their gender identity by doing what they would do anyway – namely, copying and identifying with their mother. But little boys are placed in something of a quandary, even in so-called traditional families: They are expected to disidentify with the most powerful and admired person in their small world – their mother – and, instead, to become like the parent whom they rarely see – namely, their father.

> ... In cultures where men have close relationships with children, men much less frequently affirm their masculinity through boastful demonstrations of strength, aggressiveness and sexual potency. Such cultures also are less apt to have an ideology of female inferiority, or to practice dominating behavior toward women.

Feminist object-relations theorists hold that this asymmetrical pattern of parenting is at the root of both the "reproduction of mothering" and the "reproduction of misogyny." Little girls, strongly bonded to their mothers and not required to disidentify with them just when their gender identity is being consolidated, tend to grow up with more "permeable" ego-boundaries and a greater desire to stay connected to specific others, including children of their own. But this is not an unmixed blessing for it may result in the under-development of more abstract civic virtues – such as the ability to set aside particular kin loyalties in order to apply wider standards of justice when appropriate. These are virtues that liberal feminists have been insisting for the past two centuries are women's right and duty to cultivate.

But little boys in this situation of asymmetrical parenting are forced to develop their sense of gender identity in the virtual absence of a same-sex caretaker. As a result, they are apt to conclude that "becoming a man" means becoming as unlike women as possible. As they grow older, they are at risk of escalating this exercise in "compensatory masculinity."

At worst, they may scorn and abuse women while engaging in other anti-social acts singly or with other males.

At best, they may distance themselves from whatever they perceive to be "women's work," including the hands-on caretaking of their own children. In this way, they help to reproduce the cycle of feminized parenting and male sexism in the following generation.[46]

## Empirical Evidence

If feminist object-relations theory is correct, then some empirically-testable hypotheses follow. First, other things being equal, anti-female and hyper-masculine behaviors and attitudes should be *greatest* in families and cultures where the caretaking of young children most strongly is avoided by men. Oppositely, *low* levels of male sexism and compensatory masculinity – among younger and older males alike – will be likeliest in famiļes and cultures where there is active, nurturant and appropriately authoritative (as opposed to authoritarian) father involvement in child care.

Empirical research in both pre-industrial and industrial societies supports both these hypotheses. The most extensive work on pre-industrial societies has been done by University of California sociologist Scott Coltrane, who examined coded ethnographic records of a representative sample of close to 100 cultures. He found that the cultures where fathers show the most affection, proximity and responsibility for routine child care also are the ones that are likely to have female participation in community decision-making and female access to positions of authority.[47]

In a further study, Coltrane also found that in cultures where men have close relationships with children, men much less frequently affirm their masculinity through boastful demonstrations of strength, aggressiveness and sexual potency. Such cultures also are less apt to have an ideology of female inferiority or to practice dominating behavior toward women.[48]

Another body of research done in industrial countries confirms the importance of nurturant fathering for girls – not (as older Freudian and functionalist theories would have it) in order to teach their daughters "feminine roles" and "women's place," but to help them value achievement and not engage in self-destructive *hyperfeminine* behavior. Work comparing the social behavior of adolescent girls from intact, divorced and mother-widowed homes is quite telling. In these studies, girls from intact homes related naturally and confidently to their male peers and to adult males, while girls whose fathers had died tended to be shy and inhibited around male peers and older males.

But girls from divorced families much more were likely to seek out male peers and act seductively toward them. They engaged in more and earlier sex than the other two groups of girls and a follow-up study showed that they were more apt to marry early, inappropriately, and with a greater risk of divorce.[49]

As one reviewer of this literature put it, "Deprived of a

stable relationship with a nonexploitative adult male who loves them, these girls can remain developmentally 'stuck,' struggling with issues of security and trust that well-fathered girls have already successfully resolved."[50] Or as another researcher in this area summarized it:

> The self's voice in these young women may remain fixed on one basic set of questions ... "What do I need to do, and who do I need to be, to find a man who won't abandon me, as the men in my life and my mother's life have done?" ... Girls for whom basic acceptance and love are the primary motivating forces have little interest or emotional energy to invest in school or work-related activities unless they are exceptionally bright or talented. Even then, the pull of unmet affiliative or dependency needs may be more powerful than anything the worlds of school or work have to offer.[51]

> If boys can't get acceptance from their fathers, then they are dependent on the company of other men to overwhelm the fathers' rejecting voices or the echoing sound of paternal silence.

## Why Are Fathers Important?

These findings argue strongly for heterosexual co-parenting as a core norm – that is, the roughly equal distribution of hands-on child care between fathers and mothers. Moreover, if boys are at risk of defensive masculinity in "traditional" homes where fathers are absent *much* of the time, how much more at risk will they be in homes where fathers do not live *at all*?

As might be expected, however, this conclusion has not gone unchallenged by postmodern researchers who endorse an unlimited diversity of family forms. For example, psychologist Joseph Pleck claims that the root problem is not the absence of fathers, but the traditional practice of imposing rigid gender roles on boys and girls. Thus, he concludes, if cultural ideas about what is appropriately "masculine" were to become more flexible, boys raised by women would not *need* to be hypermasculine in order to prove their manhood, as it would be perfectly acceptable for "real men" to be empathic, caring and emotionally connected.[52]

Feminist object-relations theorists certainly would not disagree that rigidly-stereotyped roles contribute to misogyny and other forms of exaggerated masculinity. But as clinician Myriam Miedzian points out, the anthropological, psychological and sociological data suggest that it largely is the *lack* of paternal involvement that *produces* rigid, dichotomous and hierarchical gender roles in the first place. "It may well be," she writes, "that male involvement in nurturant fathering is a *condition* of more fluid sex roles and decreased [male] violence."[53] This is a conjecture that future research may increasingly support as the effects of postmodern, pluralized family forms filter down to the next generation.

> Children of both sexes need to live with stable, nurturant, adult role-models of both sexes to better develop a secure gender identity that (paradoxically) then allows them to relate to each other primarily as human beings, rather than as reduced, gender-role caricatures.

But what exactly is it about involved fathering that lessens the risk of male violence and other forms of hypermasculinity in sons? This still is something of a theoretical mystery because, until recently, "parenting" effectively was equated with "mothering" and studies on the nature and dynamics of fathering were rare. Nonetheless, a preliminary reading of the available literature suggests that nurturant, appropriately-

authoritative fathering operates in two complementary ways.
Negatively, an involved fatherly presence acts as a check
on boys' aggressiveness as they grow older, something that
mothers cannot do quite as easily, however well motivated
they are. Indeed, for some educational activists in the
African-American community, urban boys raised by single
mothers need single-sex classrooms with male teachers to
help fill this gap. In these settings, black male teachers provide firm discipline and model the virtues of learning and
self-restraint. The goal is to forestall the hypermasculine
behaviors that have helped make murder the leading cause of
death for black males over 10 years of age, placed more
young black men in prison than in college, and contributed to
casual attitudes about parenting responsibilities. Knowing the
hazards and temptations of growing up male, adult men can
contribute to the socialization of young boys simply by seeing through them more readily and by being willing to con-
front and redirect hypermasculine "acting out" before it
reaches epidemic proportions.

More important, however, are the *positive* effects that
involved fathers can have. By reassuring their sons that they
are valued and loved as unique individuals, fathers implicitly
can certify them "masculine enough" to get on with the more
important business of being human. In other words, nurturant
fathering helps relieve sons of the anxiety of "proving themselves" adequately masculine by engaging in truculent and
misogynist activities and, thus, can help free their energies
for the acquistion of more adaptive – and less rigidly gender-
stereotyped – relational and work skills.

Psychologist Frank Pittman has been especially perceptive
about this second, positive aspect of fathering. Drawing on
three decades as a counselor to men struggling with identity
issues, he writes:

> Most boys nowadays are growing up with fathers who
> spend little, if any, time with them. Ironically, when the
> boy most needs to practice being a man, his father is off

somewhere playing at being a boy ... Instead of real-life
fathers, boys grow up with myths of fathers, while mothers, whatever their significance out there in the world,
reign supreme at home in the life of the boy. If fathers
have run out on mothers, in any of the many ways men
use to escape women, then boys can't imagine that their
masculinity is sufficient until they too run away from
women and join the world of men ... Boys who don't
have fathers they know and love don't know how much
masculinity is enough.

Fathers have the authority to let boys relax the require-
ments of the masculine model. If our fathers accept us, then
that declares us masculine enough to join the company of
men. In effect, boys then have their diplomas in masculinity
and can go on to develop other skills. A boy may spend his
entire life seeking that acceptance, the love and approval of
his father, and with it a reprieve from masculine striving. If
boys can't get acceptance from their fathers, then they are
dependent on the company of other men to overwhelm the
fathers' rejecting voices or the echoing sound of paternal
silence.[54]

## Conclusion

One legitimately might ask at this point if mothers are not
equally important in light of these twin processes of certify-
ing children "masculine enough" and "feminine enough."
Indeed they are; still, it is not mother absence from families
but father absence (physical and/or psychological) that has
been the greater problem in most societies, and in ours especially since the Industrial Revolution. And the bottom line
appears to be this: Children of both sexes need to live with
stable, nurturant adult role models of both sexes to better
develop a secure gender identity that (paradoxically) then
allows them to relate to each other primarily as human
beings, rather than as reduced, gender-role caricatures. This
does not require that such role models always and only be the

child's biological parents, but it strongly suggests that there are limits to the diversity of family forms that we should encourage around the core norm of heterosexual, egalitarian co-parenting.

The literature on divorce that I have reviewed is quite clear about the benefits of intact, two-parent families. The literature on homosexual parenting is less clear simply because of the recency of this phenomenon and the less-than-well-controlled research on it. However, other research, both intra- and cross-cultural, underlines the importance of fathers both to sons' and daughters' development without gainsaying the importance of mothers, as well.

As our culture has rushed to embrace first a liberal then a postmodern model of marriage, we have had to learn some lessons the hard way. In a sense, stable marriages and families are like the vitamins and minerals in healthy food. It is easy to take vitamin C for granted and not even notice its benefits until you are citrus-deprived and come down with a case of scurvy.

To pursue the metaphor, we could say that our culture has been eating relational junk food for the past 30 years and only now is beginning to acknowledge the effects. Having begun to do so, the next challenge to face is that of providing the resources for the strengthening heterosexual marriage and family life. Here we have yet another emerging body of research to help us[55] – but to go into that would be the subject of another paper!

*Mary Stewart Van Leeuwen is professor of psychology and philosophy at Eastern College, St. Davids, Pa., and resident scholar at its Hestenes Center for Christian Women in Leadership. Among her previously-published books are* Gender And Grace, After Eden *and* Religion, Feminism and the Family.

# Endnotes

1. For a more philosophical discussion of these issues from a Reformed Christian perspective, see Richard J. Mouw and Sander Griffioen, *Pluralisms and Horizons: An Essay in Christian Public Philosophy* (Grand Rapids: Eerdmans, 1993). For a discussion in the context of marriage and family, see Mary Stewart Van Leeuwen, *Gender and Grace: Love, Work and Parenting in a Changing World* (Downers Grove IL: Intervarsity, 1990), and also Anne Carr and Mary Stewart Van Leeuwen, eds., *Religion, Feminism and the Family* (Louisville: Westminster John Knox, 1996).

2. Judith Stacey, *Brave New Families: Stories of Domestic Upheaval in Late Twentieth-Century America* (New York:Basic Books, 1990). See also her chapter on "Gay and Lesbian Families: Queer Like Us" in Mary Ann Mason, Arlene Skolnick and Stephen D. Sugarman, eds. *All Our Families: New Policies for a New Century* (New York: Oxford 1998), pp. 117-43.

3. Diane Ehrensaft, *Parenting Together: Men and Women Sharing the Care of Their Children* (Urbana IL: University of Illinois Press, 1987), p. xi.

4. For a more detailed discussion of the history of the doctrine of separate spheres, see Carr and Van Leeuwen, *Op. cit.*, especially ch. 7-12. See also Carl Degler, *At Odds: Women and the Family in America from the Revolution to the Present* (New York: Oxford, 1980).

5. "In the image of God he created them; male and female he created them. God blessed them and said to them 'Be fruitful and multiply, and fill the earth and subdue it; and have dominion over the fish of the sea and over the birds of the air and over every living thing that moves upon the earth" (Gen. 1:26-28, NRSV).

6. "Committee to Study Physical, Emotional and Sexual Abuse," Report No. 30 to the Synod of the Christian Reformed Church in North America (Grand Rapids: C.R.C. Publications, 1992), pp. 313-58.

7. The Religion, Culture and Family Project, based at the University of Chicago Divinity School, has produced a series of books defending the core norm of "the public-private, two-parent family guided by a love ethic of equal regard." For a more detailed discussion of this concept, see Don S. Brown-

ing, Bonnie J. Miller-McLemore, Pamela D. Couture, K. Brynolf Lyon, and Robert M. Franklin, *From Culture Wars to Common Ground: Religion and the American Family Debate* (Louisville: Westminster John Knox, 1997). Other books in the Religion, Culture and Family Series (also from Westminster John Knox) include Carr and Van Leeuwen, *Op. cit.*, Phyllis D. Airhart and Margaret L. Bendroth, eds. *Faith Traditions and the Family* (1996); Leo G. Perdue, Joseph Blenkinsopp, John J. Collins and Carol Meyers, *Families in Ancient Israel* (1997); Carolyn Osiek and David L. Balch, *Families in the New Testament World: Households and House Churches* (1997); Ted Peters, *For the Love of Children: Genetic Technology and the Future of the Family* (1996); Max L. Stackhouse, *Covenant and Commitments: Faith, Family and Economic Life* (1997); John Witte Jr., *From Sacrament to Contract: Marriage, Religion and Law in the Western Tradition* (1997); Herbert Anderson, Don Browning, Ian Evison and Mary Stewart Van Leeuwen, eds. *The Family Handbook* (1998); and also Lisa Sowle Cahill, *Sex, Gender and Christian Ethics* (Cambridge University Press, 1996). For further information, contact the project co-ordinator at the Unviersity of Chicago Divinity School, Swift Hall, 1025 E. 58th St. Chicago IL 60637.

8. Arlene Skolnick, "Solomon's Children: The New Biologism, Psychological Parenthood, Attachment Theory and the Best Interests Standard," in Mason, Skolnick and Sugarman, *Op. cit.*, pp. 236-55.

9. For example, David Popenoe, *Life Without Father* (New York: The Free Press, 1996).

10. For example, Don S. Browning, "Biology, Ethics, and Narrative in Christian Family Theory," in David Popenoe, Jean Bethke Elshtain, and David Blankenhorn, *Promises to Keep: Decline and Renewal of Marriage in America* (Lanham MD: Rowman and Littlefield, 1996), pp. 119-56.

11. David Popenoe, for example, uses this theory of "biological stinginess" to explain patterns of stepparent disengagement and abuse of stepchildren, and to argue for policies which would strengthen marriage and make divorce – and hence the risk of children's later exposure to stepparents – less likely. See also Robert Wright, *The Moral Animal: The New Science of Evolutionary Psychology* (New York: Pantheon, 1994), and

Mary Ann Mason, "The Modern American Stepfamily: Problems and Possibilities," in Mason *et al., Op. cit.*, pp. 95-116. For some writers of a liberal bent (e.g., Wright) this doctrine of "inclusive fitness" helps make evolutionary sense of homosexuality. Single gay persons may not get half their genes into the next generation by direct reproduction, but they often help support their siblings' children, thus making it more likely that at least a quarter of their genes will survive in nieces and nephews. Evolutionary psychologists compare this to the efforts spent by sexless drones in a beehive as they serve the queen bee, who in reproducing her own genes also reproduces a portion of theirs. See for example Martin Daly and Margo Wilson, *Sex, Evolution and Behavior*, 2nd ed. (Belmont CA: Wadsworth, 1983).

12. This is said to be particularly important for men, whose evolutionary heritage has left them with two competing genetic strategies. The first is said to be that of the "cad" (i.e., the male who inseminates as many women as possible on the assumption that at least some of these will carry his genes to reproductive adulthood even in his absence). The second is that of the "dad" (i.e., the male who remains monogamous and stays with one mate and her children to help raise them to maturity). Family studies scholars of an evolutionary bent who are concerned about family stability contend that this means we must strengthen the second of these tendencies at the expense of the first.

13. Geoffrey W. Bromiley, *God and Marriage* (Grand Rapids: Eerdmans, 1980), pp. 2-3. See also Van Leeuwen, Gender and Grace, ch. 9 and Rodney Clapp, *Families at the Crossroad: Beyond Traditional and Modern Options* (Downers Grove: Intervarsity, 1990).

14. However, some Christians have absorbed this lesson incompletely. Among members of my own Calvinist denomination, it was not uncommon even through the 1980s for some to argue that adopted infants should not be baptized, since (it was argued) God maintained his covenant through the biological reproduction of his people, just as he did in the Old Testament.

15. David Orgon Coolidge, "Same-Sex Marriage?" (Wynnewood, PA: Evangelicals for Social Action, Crossroads Monograph Series on Faith and Public Policy, Vol. 1, No. 9), pp. 31-50.

See also his "Same Sex-Marriage? *Baehr v. Mike* and the Meaning of Marriage," *South Texas Law Review*, Vol. 38, No. 1 (Mar. 1997), pp 1-119. See also Mary Stewart Van Leeuwen, "To Ask a Better Question: The Heterosexuality/Homosexuality Debate Revisited," *Interpretation*, Vol. 51, No 2 (Apr. 1997), pp. 143-58.

16. See also John Witte, Jr. >*From Sacrament to Contract: Marriage, Religion and Law in the Western Tradition* (Louisville: Westminster John Knox, 1997). It should be noted that when Coolidge uses the term "traditional" marriage, he is not endorsing the doctrine of separate spheres, and would make the same three theological qualifiers that I have made.

17. For further discussion of the concept of sphere sovereignty, see L. Kalsbeek, *Contours of a Christian Philosophy* (Toronto: Wedge, 1975); Brian J. Walsh and J. Richard Middleton, *The Transforming Vision: Shaping a Christian World View* (Downers Grove IL: Intervarsity, 1984); or Albert Wolters, *Creation Regained: Biblical Basics for a Reformational Worldview* (Grand Rapids: Eerdmans, 1985).

18. David Orgon Coolidge, "The Dilemma of Same-Sex Marriage," *Crisis*, July/August 1996, pp. 17-20 (quotation from p. 18). Feminist adherents of the Liberal Model regard the old Complementarity Model with suspicion, as it has been associated in the past with men's domination of women, sexually and economically. However, as I have pointed out in the first part of this essay, one must distinguish between a creationally good marriage structures and the fallen uses to which they have been put.

19. Under this emerging model, an individual cannot go so far as to unilaterally choose whom to marry: that is still supposed to be a consensual decision. However, the individual *can* quite unilaterally choose to divorce for any or no reason whatsoever. At the same time, rates of unilaterally imposed sexual activity (date rape, sexual harassment, sexual abuse) continue to rise. Could there be a causal connection here? If one can legally leave a marriage and sexual partner on a whim, without the other person's consent, why should it not be assume that unilateral sexual imposition is not also acceptable?

20. Judith Stacey, "Gay and Lesbian Families: Queer Like Us," in Mason, Skolnick and Sugarman, *Op. cit.*, pp. 117-43 (quota-

tion from p. 129; my italics).

21. Andrew Cherlin, *Marriage, Divorce and Remarriage*, 2nd ed. (Cambridge MA: Harvard University Press, 1992). Divorce rates are expressed either as a percentage of the number of annual marriages or as a percentage of the total number of married women. However, a true measure of the proportion of marriages ending in divorce would require gathering data on an entire cohort of people until they die, which is a difficult and costly task. So instead demographers use available data to create models that will predict the proportion of marriages likely to end in divorce. When such models predict the future failure rate of current American marriages, estimates range from a low of 44 percent to a high of 64 percent. This failure rate includes remarriages, which have an even higher likelihood of failure than first marriages. Cherlin estimates that while 30 percent of once-married women will divorce within a decade, 37 percent of remarried women will do so. See also Amy E. Black, "For the Sake of the Children: Reconstructing American Divorce Policy," (Wynnewood PA: Evangelicals for Social Action, Crossroads Monograph Series on Faith and Public Policy, Vol. 1, No.2, 1995).

22. William J. Goode, *World Changes in Divorce Patterns* (New Haven CT: Yale University Press,, 1993), p. 345 (his italics).

23. For a further discussion of these historical trends, see Barbara Dafoe Whitehead, *The Divorce Culture* (New York: Knopf, 1997).

24. Joseph Epstein, *Divorced in America* (New York: E. P. Dutton, 1974), p. 18.

25. Judith S. Wallerstein and Sandra Blakeslee, *Second Chances: Men, Women and Children a Decade After Divorce* (Boston: Houghton Mifflin, 1989); see also her chapter in Mason, Skolnick and Sugarman, *Op. cit.*, "Children of Divorce: A Society in Search of a Policy," pp. 66-94.

26. See David Blankenhorn, *Fatherless America: Confronting Our Most Urgent Social Problem* (New York: Basic Books, 1995), especially ch. 10 for a review of the pertinent literature.

27. See Eleanor E. Maccoby and Robert H. Mnookin, *Dividing the Child: Social and Legal Dilemmas of Custody* (Cambridge MA: Harvard University Press, 1992), and for a more general review of this literature, Whitehead, *Op. cit.*, especially ch. 3-

5.

28. Sara S. McLanahan and Gary D. Sandefur, *Growing Up With A Single Parent: What Hurts and What Helps* (Cambridge: Harvard University Press, 1994).

29. Wallerstein, "Children of Divorce," pp. 71, 73.

30. See Wallerstein, *Second Chances*, pp. 226-28 and Mary Ann Mason, "The Modern American Stepfamily: Problems and Possibilities," in Mason, Skolnick and Sugarman, *Op. cit.*, pp. 95-116. Using American data, Mason reports (p. 116) that "about one-quarter of all remarrying women separate from their new spouses within five years of the second marriage, and the figure is higher for women with children from prior relationships. A conservative estimate is that between 20 and 30 percent of stepchildren will, before they turn eighteen, see their custodial parent and stepparent divorce. This is yet another disruptive marital transition for children, most of whom have already undergone one divorce."

31. Norval D. Glenn, "Values, Attitudes and the State of American Marriage," in David Popenoe, Jean Bethke Elshtain and David Blankenhorn, eds., *Promises to Keep: Decline and Renewal of Marriage in America* (Lanham MD: Rowman and Littlefield, 1996), pp. 15-33 (quotation from p. 32).

32. For a summary of this literature, see Hilary Lips, *Sex and Gender: An Introduction*, 3rd ed. (Mountain View CA: Mayfield, 19970, especially ch. 9.

33. Norval Glenn specifically acknowledges that this is the case, despite overall the downward decline of *reported* marital satisfaction. "As a whole, persons in satisfactory marriages are happier, healthier, more productive, and are less inclined to engage in socially disruptive behavior than other adults, and at least among persons beyond the earliest stages of adulthood, there is no evidence of appreciable decline in these differences." (in Glenn, "Values, Attitudes and American Marriage," pp. 21-22).

34. Linda Waite, "Does Marriage Matter?" *Demography*, Vol. 32, No. 4 (Nov. 1995), pp. 483-507.

35. Linda J. Waite, "Social Science Finds: 'Marriage Matters'", *The Responsive Community*, Vol. 6, No. 3 (Summer 1996), pp. 26-35 (quotation from p. 33)

36. Judith Stacey points out, quite correctly, that the shift among both feminists and gays to a positive view of "marriage" is a shift from the 1960s and 1970s, when marriage was seen as an institution oppressive to both women and gays, and therefore to be avoided, if not completely eliminated. There are many reasons for this shift, of which disillusionment with the liberal model as a result of personal experience is one. However, there is still internal dissent in both feminist and gay movements on this issue, with some still adhering to a liberal model of no-fault divorce and serial monogamy, and others romanticizing sexual freedom and even childbearing with no covenantal partnering at all. See Stacey's "Gay and Lesbian Families" in Mason, Skolnick and Sugarman, *Op. cit.*

37. See David H. Demo and Katherine R. Allen, "Diversity Within Lesbian and Gay Families: Challenges and Implications for Family Theory and Research," *Journal of Social and Personal Relationships*, Vol. 13, No. 3 (1996) pp. 415-34. It should be also noted that although the Scandinavian countries have had legalized domestic partnerships for homosexuals since the late 1980s or early 1990s, none of them allows medically-supervised artificial insemination or adoption by couples other than married men and women.

38. There is yet a further problem in comparing heterosexual with homosexual parenting, and one which I have yet to see acknowledged in any of the methodological discussions – namely, that no attempt is made to control for the stability of the parenting relationships. In the studies of lesbian mothers, it is usually not clear whether or for how long they have been in a domestic partnership with another woman, or how many such partnerships have been entered into during the raising of the children being studied.

39. Demo and Allen, "Lesbian and Gay Families," pp. 415 & 432. One also suspects academic opportunism is at work for these researchers, given their frequent references to the "exciting opportunities for testing, revising and constructing families theories" (p 116, also pp. 422, 423, 431) that await scholars ready to study postmodern family forms.

40. Stacey, "Gay and Lesbian Families," p. 131.

41. The study is: Fiona Tasker and Susan Golombok, "Adults Raised as Children in Lesbian Families," *American Journal of*

*Orthopsychiatry*, Vol. 65, No. 2 (Apr. 1995), pp. 203-15. Although Stacey casts this as a longitudinal study because it used adult children from a sample of lesbians interviewed twenty years earlier, in fact it involved no longitudinal measures of the children themselves. As in almost all studies, these lesbian mothers were divorced women who originally had their children in heterosexual marriages. Moreover, the attrition rate between the two interview dates was over a third (only 62 percent of the original mothers interviewed agreed to let their children be contacted or interviewed as adults), thus further reducing the generalizability of the findings.

42. Stacey, "Gay and Lesbian families," pp. 132, 133.

43. See Demo and Allen, "Diversity Within Lesbian and Gay Families" for particularly strong assumptions on the compatibility homosexual parenting with feminist concerns.

44. An earlier version of this section appeared in Mary Stewart Van Leeuwen, "Opposite Sexes or Neighboring Sexes? The Importance of Gender in the Welfare Responsibility Debate," in Stanley Carlson-Thies and James Skillen, eds. *Welfare in America: Christian Perspectives on a Policy in Crisis* (Grand Rapids: Eerdmans, 1996), pp. 243-74.

45. For an exhaustive review of the theoretical and empirical work in this area, see Scott Coltrane, *Family Man: Fatherhood, Housework, and Gender Equity* (New York: Oxford, 1996). Earlier feminist accounts include Dorothy Dinnerstein, *The Mermaid and the Minotaur: Sexual Arrangements and Human Malaise* (New York: Harper Colophon, 1977); Nancy Chodorow, *The Reproduction of Mothering: Psychoanalysis and the Sociology of Gender* (Berkeley: University of California Press, 1978) and Miriam Miedzian, *Boys Will Be Boys: Breaking the Link Between Masculinity and Violence* (New York: Doubleday, 1991). See also the May 1998 theme issue of the journal *Demography* on "Men in Families."

46. It is not inconsistent with the object-relations analysis for men to alternate scorn of women with their veneration, as in cultures where women are categorized either as "madonnas" or "whores." Either strategy marginalizes women and keeps them from being seen as fellow human beings with whom men can share activity in both public and domestic realms.

47. Scott Coltrane, "Father-Child Relationships and the Status of Women: A Cross-Cultural Study," *American Journal of Sociology*, Vol. 93, No. 1 (Mar. 1988), pp. 1060-95.

48. Scott Coltrane, "The Micropolitics of Gender in Nonindustrial Societies," *Gender and Society*, Vol. 6, No. 1 (Mar. 1992), pp. 86-107.

49. E. Mavis Hetherington, "Effects of Father Absence on Personality Development of Adolescent Daughters," *Developmental Psychology*, Vol. 7, No. 3 (1972), pp. 313-26. See also Patricia Draper and Henry Harpending, "Father Absence and Reproductive Strategy: An Evolutionary Perspective," *Journal of Anthropological Research*, Vol. 38, No. 3 (1982), pp. 255-73, and Popenoe, Life Without Father, ch. 5.

50. Blankenhorn, *Fatherless America*, p. 47.

51. Judith S. Musick, *Young, Poor and Pregnant: The Psychology of Teenage Motherhood* (New Haven CT: Yale University Press, 1993), p. 60.

52. Joseph Pleck, *The Myth of Masculinity* (Cambridge MA: M.I.T. Press, 1983).

53. Miedzian, *Boys Will Be Boys*, pp. 87-88.

54. Frank Pittman, "Beyond the B.S. and Drum-Beating: Staggering Through Life as a Man," *Psychology Today*, Vol. 25, No. 1 (Jan/Feb 1992), pp. 78-83 (quotation from pp. 82-83). See also his *Man Enough: Fathers, Sons and the Search for Masculinity* (New York: Putnam, 1993), and also Samuel Osherson, *Finding Our Fathers: How a Man's Life is Shaped by His Relationship with His Father* (New York: Fawcett, 1986) and *Wrestling With Love: How Men Struggle with Intimacy* (New York: Fawcett, 1992).

55. For starters, West and Hewlett, *Op. cit.*; John Gottman, *Why Marriages Succeed or Fail* (New York: Simon and Schuster, 1994); Mary Pipher, *The Shelter of Each Other: Rebuilding Our Families* (New York: Putnam, 1996); Judith S. Wallerstein and Sandra Blakeslee, *The Good Marriage: How and Why Love Lasts* (Boston: Houghton Mifflin, 1995).